WORDS AS GRAIN

词如谷粒

WORDS

AS

GRAIN

词如谷粒

DUO DUO

多多

New and Selected Poems

Translated from
the Chinese and Edited by

Lucas Klein

Yale
UNIVERSITY
PRESS

NEW HAVEN AND LONDON

The Margellos World Republic of Letters is dedicated to making literary works from around the globe available in English through translation. It brings to the English-speaking world the work of leading poets, novelists, essayists, philosophers, and playwrights from Europe, Latin America, Africa, Asia, and the Middle East to stimulate international discourse and creative exchange.

The poems in this collection have been selected from the Chinese publications *Nuoyan: Duo Duo ji, 1972–2012* [诺言：多多集, 1972–2012] [*Promise: Poems of Duo Duo, 1972–2012*] (Beijing: Zuojia chubanshe, 2013) and *Wangxiang shi zhenshi de zhuren* [妄想是真实的主人] [*Delusion Is the Master of Reality*] (Beijing: Yilin chubanshe, 2018).

Set in Yale and Futura type by Dustin Kilgore.
Printed in the United States of America.

Library of Congress Control Number: 2020946686
ISBN 978-0-300-22739-0 (hardcover : alk. paper)

A catalogue record for this book is available from the British Library.

This paper meets the requirements of ANSI/NISO Z39.48-1992 (Permanence of Paper).

10 9 8 7 6 5 4 3 2 1

Contents

Amsterdam's River (1989–2004)

Delusion Is the Master of Reality (1982–1988)

Instruction (1972–1976)

Translator's Introduction

How to make sense of Duo Duo's poetry is the overarching question it poses, at the root of its political significance as well as its literary interest. In the words of his 1987 poem "Remade," he has worked to "remake language with remade tools" and "with remade language / keep remaking." How should his continued remaking be read? What does the reader need in order to understand his remade language?

Duo Duo was born in Beijing in 1951 as Li Shizheng 栗世征 (he gave himself his pen name in honor of his daughter, called Duoduo, who died in infancy in 1982). He was born two years after the founding of the People's Republic of China, and his life follows its general historical outlines: he came of age during the Cultural Revolution (1966–1976), reached maturity as a poet during the "reform and opening" years of the 1980s, lived abroad during China's economic explosion in the 1990s, and returned in 2004 to a country beset by problems known in many other internationalized economies (inequality, authoritarianism, nativism, etc.). But his writing has never been reducible to a mirror of or straightforward response to the conditions of its creation.

He told me once, with only a hint of frustration, that Chinese readers tend to favor his earlier works—I think because they take his early works as expressions of the era. In contrast, I have placed the poems he has written since his return to China first in this book; the parts of the book move progressively back in time. Chinese publications tend to divide poetry by decade; this book is arranged by life period and roughly follows the decades, but not precisely. The first part, titled "The Force of Forging Words (2004–2018)," covers the period since he returned to China; "Amsterdam's River (1989–2004)" represents his exile years, which he spent mostly in the Netherlands; "Delusion Is the Master of Reality (1982–1988)" corresponds to China's "reform and opening" years; finally, "Instruction (1972–1976)" includes his earliest work, from the middle of the Cultural Revolution until the eve of the Deng Xiaoping era. I have arranged the book this way to some extent because I feel that the more the poems move into the past, the more they require contextualization for the non-Chinese reader. My introduction of Duo Duo and his works will likewise start with the present and move backward as I ask to what degree contextualization is useful in reading his poetry.

Appreciation of Duo Duo's most recent work is not helped much by knowledge of the environment in which it was produced. Though naturalized as a Dutch citizen, he returned to China in 2004 after fifteen years living abroad to teach at Hainan University, dividing his time between the southern island and Beijing. He has lived in Beijing full-time since retirement. He stays in a small apartment without a mailbox; if you want to send him something, he must be there himself to receive it. A vegetarian (and one not opposed to drinking), he has an affinity, revealed in his poetry, with the mixture of Indian Buddhism and Chinese Daoism known as Zen, with its mysteries and suspicion of language. From "To Have the Honor of Reading Shivers in the Moonlight" (2007):

> sūtra rivers reciting words of inaction
> the departed are the audience
> the audience is silence

And yet language – despite refracting what it is meant to reflect, contorting what it means to convey – is also made, constructed.

The first part of this book is titled after this 2014 poem:

The Force of Forging Words

outside force, continuing on
from enough, is insufficient hallucination

light vanishes with feathers
stillness cannot be forfended

candles stuck with wings know only to advance
what's most loved is dark and quiet

this is rationale's wasteland
but the ethics of poetry

dream and the boat on the shore must join forces
if words can spill beyond their own bounds

only there, to test the hearing of the end

Words may be inadequate, and silence may be the audience, but Duo Duo has been writing of language — and, by extension, poetry — as a made thing since 1984, when he wrote his poem "The Construction of Language Comes from the Kitchen." Here, in "The Force of Forging Words," Duo Duo acknowledges at once that what lies beyond this force is a dream, itself inadequate, and that stillness is unpreventable — even as it may be the wasteland of reasoning, if not reason itself. Stillness is also where we must look for what is ethical about poetry. These ethics are separate from solutions to the practical problems of life in a country such as China or a city such as Beijing, which do not enter his poetry much. Yet there may be something applicable in the poem's philosophy, which is for words to "spill from their own bounds," to unite the force of forging words with the force of what words forge.

Words spilling from their own bounds means that they pour out into mystery and multiplicity, but amid the multiplicity there can be room for a bit of context — context does not need to undermine what is compelling about the mysteries of Duo Duo's poetry. Duo Duo himself lived "beyond bounds" — in the UK and Canada for a time, as well as the Netherlands. He ended up abroad because he was invited to the Poetry International Festival in Rotterdam and flew from Beijing to London, where he had also arranged readings. His flight departed on June 4, 1989, but since April of that year Tiananmen Square, at the center of Beijing, had been occupied by students and workers whose commemoration of the death of reformist Communist Party leader Hu Yaobang had turned into a large-scale demonstration for democratic reforms, with hunger strikes and protests spreading to many other cities throughout China. On the night of June 3, a matter of hours before Duo Duo's flight, the military entered Beijing to crush the protests, killing an untold number (the Chinese government once reported 241 deaths; the Chinese Red Cross had estimated 2,600 but retracted it) in what would become known as the Tiananmen Square Massacre (or, within China, as the Tiananmen Incident). Duo Duo had not been known as a dissident, and his plane ticket had been booked long in advance. But he had been a witness to the demonstrations and the military suppression, and in London and Rotterdam he spoke freely to journalists about the massacre. Going home soon was not an option. The second part of this book, representing his years in exile, is titled from a poem written in the first year of that exile:

Amsterdam's River

in the November nightfall city
there is only Amsterdam's river

suddenly

the tangerines on my tree at home
shake in the autumn wind

I close the window, but no use
the river flows upstream, but no use
that sun inlaid with pearls, rising

no use
pigeons disperse like iron filings
and the streets with no boys suddenly seem so spacious

after autumn rain
the roof that's crawling with snails
— my country

slowly floats by, on Amsterdam's river

The poem is one of displacement: the home with the tangerine tree is not in Amsterdam, even as the speaker's country floats by on Amsterdam's river. And since the river is flowing upstream, things are not proceeding the way they were expected to proceed. Context provides an anchor: in the line about streets with no boys suddenly seeming so spacious, I see an image of Beijing's streets after the slaughter of the protesters.

Duo Duo was not there to see China's transformation in the nineties, but the decade was a time of exponential growth and drastic change there. In 1989, Europe and the United States put an embargo on selling arms to China; by 2000, Beijing had been awarded the 2008 Summer Olympics. In 1992, the paramount leader of China, Deng Xiaoping, made a tour of the south of China, including his Special Economic Zones, such as Shenzhen (then a city of 1.3 million, today a city of over 12 million), called for the development of the Pudong region of Shanghai (now the city's most populous area, in addition to being the location of its financial district and most famous skyscrapers), and proclaimed "To get rich is glorious." Duo Duo's "Courtyard Home" (1999) contains the following lines:

> stone coffin wood cart ancient road urban infrastructure
>
> over the ridges of low-rise roofs, the logic of
> the courtyard home, street grids, whose
> palmprint prophesied it into a square

The poem reads like an attempt to work through news of China and its changes in relation to what Duo Duo remembered. A poem such as this must have been psychologically necessary for him to return to China a few years later. The "square" here is not the shape but a city square, such as Tiananmen.

If there is a tension between these two ways of reading Duo Duo's poetry—reading them for the arguments they make about eternal concepts or else looking for the contexts provided by his life experiences and seeing how the contexts might ground what the poems say—then to some extent Duo Duo's own poetry can offer an answer. The third part of this book borrows its title from a poem written in 1982:

and we, we are birds touching lip to lip
in the story of time
undertaking our final division
from man

the key turns in the ear
the shadows have left us
the key keeps turning
birds are reduced to people
people unacquainted with birds

The poem prizes the abstract and ethereal: birds, which are ungrounded; stories, which are removed representations; shadows . . . and yet the shadows have left us, and the birds are reduced to people who do not know what they were reduced from. If delusion is the master of reality, if we do not want the birds of our reading reduced to the point where we are unable to understand the ungrounded and airborne, then perhaps the best way to read a poem is for our own thoughts to drift from the words provided and master the reality of the poem with our fantasy, with our imagination. After all, our thoughts will control what we understand more than objective reality will offer us truth from facts.

At the same time, to proclaim delusion the master of reality seems to argue against the possibility of "seeking truth from facts" — Deng Xiaoping's slogan in promoting his brand of socialism as more pragmatic than Chairman Mao Zedong's had been. To seek truth from facts is pointless, Duo Duo's poem implies, if facts, or reality, are mastered by someone or other's deluded sense of truth. Does contextualizing the poem this way, according to the facts of when it was written, counter the logic of the poem? Nevertheless, the eighties were days of optimism and idealism, of "high culture fever" and debates about "Obscure Poetry" – poetry affiliated with *Jintian* (Today), the first unofficial literary journal in the People's Republic when it went to print in 1978 – by poets such as Bei Dao (b. 1949), Mang Ke (b. 1950), Shu Ting (b. 1952), Yang Lian (b. 1955), and Gu Cheng (1956–1993). These poets became minor celebrities not only because distractions like televisions were rare but also because they wrote work that, in contrast to what little had been available before, rewarded rereading and instigated imagination. For a time, believing they were the masters of reality did not seem delusional.

In the even earlier era, a different kind of delusion ruled reality. The final part of this book is titled after a poem from 1976:

Instruction

– a decadent memorial

in just one night, the wound burst
and all the books on the bookshelf betrayed them
only the era's greatest singer
with a hoarse voice, at ear-side, sang softly:
    night of jazz, night of a century
they were eliminated by the forests of an advanced society
and limited to such themes:
to appear only as a foil to the
world's miseries, miseries
that would become their lives' obligation

who says the themes of their early lives
were bright, even today they still take it
as a harmful dictum
on a night with no artistic storyline
lamplight originated in misperception
what they saw was always

a monotonous rope appearing in winter's snowfall
they could only keep playing, tirelessly
wrestling with whatever flees and living
with whatever cannot remember
even if it brought back their earliest longings
emptiness became the stain on their lives

their misfortune came from the misfortune of ideals
but their pain they'd helped themselves to
self-consciousness sharpened their thinking
but from self-consciousness, blood loss
they couldn't make peace with tradition
even though the world had existed
uncleanly a long time before their birth
still they wanted to find
whichever first criminal discovered "truth"
and tear down the world
and all the time it needed to wait

faced with chains hanging around their necks
their only crazy act
was pulling them tighter
but they were no comrades
their disparate destructive forces
were never close to grabbing society's attention
and they were reduced to being spiritual criminals
because: they had abused allegory

yet in the end, they pray in the classroom of thought
and fall comatose at seeing their own handwriting so clearly:
the time they lived in was not the one the lord had arranged
they are the misborn, stopped at the point of
    misunderstanding life

and all they went through – nothing but the tragedy of
  being born

Written at the end of the Cultural Revolution, the poem tells the story of the urban youths who were at first at the forefront of the era but soon became its victims, betrayed by their bookshelves: their misfortune was that of their ideals, and their self-consciousness resulted in blood loss and an inability to make peace with tradition, for they had to live lives of arrested development, their tragedy nothing but the tragedy of being born.

Here some knowledge of Duo Duo's life and times may be helpful. The Cultural Revolution began with Mao's attempt to rid the Party of suspected capitalists and its entrenched bureaucracy. For this he mobilized students to agitate not only against the Party, of which he was chairman, but, by extension, against anyone in a position of authority, including teachers. Schools were shut down, and China's educated young formed themselves into factions of Red Guards. Duo Duo was of this generation, and his formal education ended halfway through high school (given his intellectual family background, he was deemed insufficiently "Red" to become a Red Guard). Mao changed course in 1968 and called on urban students to move to rural villages, ostensibly to learn from the peasantry but also to get them out of the way as the military reimposed order on the country. This is how the educated youths were betrayed by their books.

Duo Duo was sent to Baiyangdian, in Hebei province, ninety-three miles south of Beijing, along with his high school friends Mang Ke and Yue Zhong (known as Genzi, b. 1951). They became known among poetry readers as the Three Musketeers of Baiyangdian; in an essay from 1988, "The Buried Poets," Duo Duo refers to the village as "a cradle." In 1969, Minister of Defense Lin Biao was named vice-chairman of the Party, and the military took control of the country, but within the Party's central committee there were tensions between Lin's military, civilian radicals under the leadership of Mao's wife Jiang Qing, and more pragmatic officials, such as Prime Minister Zhou Enlai. After a failed coup by Lin Biao (or, more likely, his subordinates), Lin allegedly fled the country and died in a plane crash in Mongolia, resulting in intensified political struggles between Jiang Qing's radical faction and the Zhou Enlai–led pragmatists. As for the youths, "emptiness became the stain on their lives // their misfortune came from the misfortune of ideals."

When Zhou died in 1976, he was mourned in large-scale demonstrations featuring poetry readings – not experimental or underground poetry, but then these poets' "disparate destructive forces / were never close to grabbing society's attention." When Mao died in September, eight months later, Jiang Qing and her allies made a last-ditch power grab, but within months they were arrested, labeled by the military as the Gang of Four, and made to bear the blame for the tumult of the preceding years (in fact, their first charges were for "undermining" the Cultural Revolution). In 1978, Deng Xiaoping took the reins of the country and instituted the era of "reform and opening."

In his "Buried Poets" essay, Duo Duo says his life as a poet began when a fragment came to him: "the window opens like an eye." He had been reading Salinger and Sartre in clandestine editions, published for "internal circulation" among high-level Communist cadres. He remembers the date: June 19, 1972. It was the year after the plane crash that killed Lin Biao and only months after Richard Nixon's visit to China. To some extent, the changing times must have opened his eyes, just as some knowledge of what Duo Duo and China have gone through can open our eyes as readers. But even if context does help explain some of Duo Duo's poetry, and where he and his writing come from, it cannot answer all the questions the poems toss up. The first poem in the last part – and one of the first poems Duo Duo saved, the first poem to open many of his retrospective publications – is titled "When the People Stand Up from Cheese" (1972). It reads:

> song omits the bloodiness of revolution
> August is like a cruel bow
> the poison boy walks out of the commune
> with tobacco and a dry throat
> livestock wear barbaric blinders
> blackened corpses hanging over their butts like swollen drums
> until the sacrifice behind the hedge eventually blurs
> and far away, more smoking troops embark

At one level, the poem gives voice to a startling expression of Red Guard ideological fallout. Everything is violent or else the passive result of violence, like charred corpses and smoke-dried throats. Yet the title is a mystery: the image of people "standing up" echoes Chairman Mao's proclamation that with the victory of the Communist Party in 1949 the people of China had "stood up" (though to say so is to ignore the bloodiness of their standing). But to stand up "from cheese"? The word adds an absurdity to the depiction of Cultural Revolutionary pessimism. Perhaps the foreign foodstuff implies some of the foreign origins of Duo Duo's poetics? He later defined the awakening he experienced when he read Baudelaire's phrase "The sun is like a poet," a contrast with "Chairman Mao is like the sun," a line in a song he had grown up with. Or maybe *ganlao*, which I have translated as "cheese," is *aaruul*, the dried curds eaten in Inner Mongolia. That might make more sense given the agricultural setting of the poem, with its livestock and farm communes. Then again, scholars have claimed *ganlao* 干酪 to be a misprint for *ganhan* 干鼾, or "dry snoring." And yet in Duo Duo's publications in China, it is still printed as "cheese," *ganlao*. So the reader must either find a way to make sense of it or yield to its senselessness.

As a translator, I must both make sense of his poetry and yield to its transcendence of sense. The questions through which I have traced this introduction to Duo Duo's work—namely, whether the poems are best read as tied to their contexts or as independent works of the imagination—are the same questions we must ask of translations: are they best approached as if tethered to the texts they are representing, or can they take on lives of their own in a new language? In both cases, I hope that the answer is *both*. I must make sense of Duo Duo's words and interpret them, but I have not tried to unpack or interpret or impose any deeper meanings. That is the task of the reader, not the translator.

While I believe in the potential of readers to come up with their own readings, and the potential of poems in translation thereby to take on lives of their own, I also demand accuracy. I have aimed to put in English what he has put in Chinese, the way he has put it. There is enough mystery in his images and how they interact and interlock that I see no need to mystify the Chinese language he writes in (as his poems argue, the mystery is in all language, any language). Attentiveness to the syntax and vocabulary of Chinese can resolve some of the apparent ambiguities or obscurities in his poetry—to allow other ambiguities to develop more fully. For instance, the opening couplet of "Amsterdam's River" reads, *shiyi yue ruye de chengshi / wei you Amusitedan de heliu* 十一月入夜的城市 / 唯有阿姆斯特丹的河流. At the center of the first line is *ruye* 入夜, which character by character would mean "enter night"—making the line something like, "November / enter night / city." At first I was confused: "city of November entering night"? "the city that enters night in November"? Is the city entering night or the month? How? But then I realized that *ruye* is simply a word on its own, meaning "nightfall." (Imagine someone over-poeticizing the line in English, or misunderstanding it, to wonder whether November or the city was "falling" into night.) Hence my translation: "in the November nightfall city / there is only Amsterdam's river" (whether "river" should be singular or plural sent me to maps of the Netherlands: there are many canals in Amsterdam but only one river, the Amstel).

But translation is not only about getting the words right according to their dictionary definitions. Attentiveness on the translator's behalf to the specifics of the imagery can clarify potential confusions. "Amsterdam's River" also contains the line *gequn xiang tiexie sanluo* 鸽群像铁屑散落. The word *gequn* 鸽群 can refer to a flock of doves or pigeons; Chinese does not differentiate between the two, so the translator must decide. It is common, of course, for poets to write about doves — they have the same symbolism in modern Chinese that they have in English — but the birds in question are being compared to *tiexie* 铁屑, "shaved iron," and so are not white but gray brown. The line reads "pigeons disperse like iron filings" in my translation.

My goal as both translator and compiler of the poems included here is to let Duo Duo's style come through. A "new and selected" anthology, it includes every poem Duo Duo has published since his last collection in English translation, plus a selection of his poetry of the previous three decades. His previous books of poetry in English translation are *Statements: The New Chinese Poetry of Duoduo* (Wellsweep, 1989), with translations by John Cayley and Gregory B. Lee; an expanded and corrected edition of *Statements* titled *Looking Out from Death: From the Cultural Revolution to Tiananmen Square* (Bloomsbury, 1989); *Crossing the Sea: Poems in Exile / Poems in China* (House of Anansi, 1998), translated by Lee Robinson and Li Ming Yu; and *The Boy Who Catches Wasps* (Zephyr Press, 2002), translated by Gregory B. Lee. To avoid overlapping too much with earlier anthologies in English, I offer some poems they do not include, retranslate some poems they have already made available, and leave out other poems. My sources are the poems published in Duo Duo's most recent career-spanning collections, *Promise* 诺言 (Zuojia chubanshe, 2013) and *Delusion Is the Master of Reality* 妄想是真实的主人 (Yilin chubanshe, 2018), as well as Duo Duo himself, who provided me with a number of more recent poems.

The most thorough scholarly work on Duo Duo in English is *Language Shattered: Contemporary Chinese Poetry and Duoduo,* by Maghiel van Crevel (Research School CNWS, Leiden University, 1996), which not only includes readings of Duo Duo's poetry up to its publication but also presents a comprehensive history of underground poetry in mainland China from the sixties onward. Other books with significant scholarly treatment of Duo Duo's work are *Contemporary Chinese Literature: From the Cultural Revolution to the Future,* by Yibing Huang (Palgrave Macmillan, 2007); and *Troubadours, Trumpeters, Troubled Makers: Lyricism, Nationalism and Hybridity in China and Its Others* (Duke University Press, 1996) and *China's Lost Decade* (Zephyr, 2012), both by Gregory B. Lee. Lee also describes details of Duo Duo's life leading up to and immediately after the Tiananmen Square Massacre in his remembrance, "Tiananmen: Lives of the Poets," published in the June 2019 issue of the online *Cha: An Asian Literary Journal.* Duo Duo's fiction, translated by John A. Crespi, has also been published as *Snow Plain: Selected Stories* (Zephyr, 2010). For a translation of the Duo Duo essay I referred to as "The Buried Poets," see "Underground Poetry in Beijing 1970–1978," translated by John Cayley, in *Under-sky, Underground,* edited by Henry Y. H. Zhao and John Cayley (WellSweep, 1994), pp. 97–104. Duo Duo won the prestigious Neustadt International Prize for Literature in 2010, and he was featured in the March–April 2011 issue of *World Literature Today,* with scholarly appreciations by Yibing Huang and Michelle Yeh. Since 2002, however, his newest work has not been available to readers of English. This book rectifies that lack.

I would like to thank Duo Duo for his enthusiasm and willingness to answer my queries and for tossing queries back at me. Thanks also to my wife, Shenxin Li, for her encouragement and for answering my many questions. I would also like to express my gratitude to Eliot Weinberger, Eleanor Goodman, Maghiel van Crevel, and Chris Song for their suggestions and support of the manuscript and, most of all, to Tammy Lai-Ming Ho for her thorough reading, corrections, and feedback.

WORDS AS GRAIN
词如谷粒

THE FORCE OF FORGING WORDS
(2004–2018)

.

The Whip Brandished on the Wheel
轮上鞭子挥舞

ah, the magnetic fields bursting out in fourteen lines
days in the soprano section, advancing grammar
wheat that stands up, acre on acre of clouds
dying together toward the west, soliciting life's representation
batch on batch, continuing investment

ah, the horse's lyrical journal – soliloquies
recoil advancing with the boat tracker's stiff accumulation
fathers layer upon layer, soliciting singers and daggers
chopping beauty taller than an axe
from atop epitaphs with the aura of wheat fields

ah rain, a cross-shaped desert in vertical
ah tears and heavy water, openly displaying the rank of the Virgin
a petroleum disposable pain, leaving back
the ditch of the military, the ditch of praise, leaving back why –
the primordial interrogation in the screams of open grasslands

ah, the whip brandished on the wheel

(2004)

Tonight We Sow
今夜我们播种

tulips, end times, and reinforcements
plus bed after bed of wheat that nourishes only two

tonight a piano made of ice and a goldfish's universal meditations
     are in synch
but the obtuse sea knows only how to rise alone

tonight the sound of wind is not limited to the air, tonight the
     quiet
cannot fool this place, tonight the church doors are closed

tonight the bowls around us all stop begging
all the gazes that surveil us meet one another

behind the clouds our secrets should be singing in public
tonight, Jesus hugs me on your body

     tonight is the night of our divorce

(2004)

A Night Configured
When Our Love Was Thickest
在我们的爱最浓时合成的夜晚

my box is very light
a sail has gently cut into the lawn
on the boat, our buildings are carried
hope presses up against our neighbors
further in the distance, parting
is composed of more newlywed homes
my box is even lighter

to advance

(2004)

In Class

上课

which means waiting is the most ancient thing
classrooms are already bending down for them

"able to hide, thus able to recite"

these heads lower even lower
to get closer to the innocent

"having read the river's lullaby"

reciting sends away more
reticence, everything agrees

"no need to read out loud"

these whose heads are buried in books
are all the further from reticence

"let the words have Sundays of their own"

(2004)

Parisian Temple

巴黎的庙

only shoes in the yard, no people seen
the ascetic's breath comes from long ago, far away

a bowl of noodles, graced with eastern thought's *adhiṣṭhāna* aura
four tangerines, aftertaste held in the mouth

the visitors go out the gate, lilies growing in their shoes
the conversations that were, taken away by the waters of the Seine

Eiffel Tower like a comma maxima
sending out long-lost sounds

no pursuit presently
no more thickness from the entering of scripture

(2004)

Listening to the Desert Poplar Grove Inside Song
听歌声中的胡杨林

snow water sent flowing
to a distance full of red tamarisks
creates white birch nervousness

— we only want one kind of jade
thus measure sand dune bewilderment

from the depths of the emerald
clouds wearing copper hats rise in great number
over our vigilance

selling continued, measuring out continued
silhouettes creep like ice floe beggars

from behind a rainbow-colored mica scrim
a high song is sent out, pleasantly resonant with
the invisible acoustics above the snow line

to the riverbank accepted by tolerance
to stop alleys of affection from crying

fritillary bulbs, wind-weeds, and yeast
crawl and unfold and expand
dyeing undulating homes

blackberries and black plums continue to weave into
sympathy, long worn through by the rug

from distances proofread by the plains
horses gallop in a tinfoil flash
grasslands struggling to get free

on the slope where the minutes and seconds run around
on the road where even light takes flight

a quick whip, with a crisp crack, pulls so far
until shovels transporting quicksand
bend into rings, and

bow replaces sickle
when shooting the harvest to further locations

and the desert poplar grove is still
on top of the wild's great restraint
speaking for fate on limitations, saying

what's far is the city, what's far is the wall
and the very far — that's the devotion that will save us

(2005)

Between Two Chestnut Forests
Is a Plot of Arable Land
两片栗林夹着一块耕地

four-cornered wind conceals affectionate speech
the funereal portrait leaves behind the spring and autumn of the
    yard
my parents are now two rows of trees with no complaints
densely interconnected with
the wilderness of depth

tidying up all the stories on the stone steps
I wish I could return to the last about-face
and see the tablecloth with goldfish print
shaking cloud-shaped life behind the chestnut grove

in the distance, people stretching their muscles
have taken my train of thought away

(2005)

White Sands Gate

白沙门

pool table against the crumbling statue, no one
giant fishnet strung up on a broken wall, no one
bicycle locked to a stone pillar, no one
angels on the pillar and three shot down, no one
the asphalt sea will soon spread over this place, no one
still a horse on the beach, but no one
you stand there and are made redundant, no one
no one, no one makes a home of standing guard —

(2005)

After Red Fingernails Have Been Sought
红指甲搜索过后

your whole night is only half a day
half total black, half black all through

rolling over in morning black, blacker convincing all black
at the time of blackest wick

what's left is only silk, teaching
us to sleep, teaching us black

tends to black in the black
life surges up again

with a black that set off long ago
to chase a new round of black

the caw of the white peacock crosses the porch
—from inception instigating black

black, a day howling initiators' ashes
black, tolerant of all hearts

black, no one walks out of this story
but black rushes out of this ordering—

(2005)

The Signaler Raises a Flag

信号员举旗

the train is lost within direction
the river that picked you up flits across the bridge
each star is shifting gears

    to be human is to be far

you pass through the sound
you pass through the same place
— the place you never entered

    the next stop is the platform

(2006)

In the Room

在屋内

in the room or in the atmosphere
you cannot walk out of this night

a drop of water a bit of time
you cannot walk out of being in:

I'm in, I'm not in
the room where there's only a bit of time:

you at your end are you, you
cannot walk out, and cannot walk back

wavering before collecting the core of the self:
anatta, no me

primary process of a white candle shedding
tears, hovering

you cannot walk out of this empty room
but see the mountain as a drifting cloud

(2006)

The Sunlight in the Art Studio
画室中的阳光

illuminate the bygone things
in the locked-up dimness of the distant past
you cannot see the hand that guides details
gods are absent

light is conserving its shine
and does not suspect amid crooked color
those points of highlight, which yet invite
the small jar on the scale, a little honey
and insect chirps, to enter together
the pupil of expanding evensong

within, more spacious than a battlefield
within, things are vanquished by emptiness

in this illumination where loss has hit its limit
see the beauty of the hand that wipes the tears
the beauty of the hand that shatters the dish

there is still tragedy, but then there is still the landscape

(2006)

Where Are You

你在哪里

stop after stop within echo
now no more than a little spot of silence
still absorbing another geography

just as without a guide, black is total
without another horizon
emptiness, too, elapses
in the place of hardening that left your death
there is no other death
above where your woman received her shock
maintaining your flying poise
— a more abundant death

when the wind from the mountain pass still threatens the already dead
when death fears the faked death
the cliff's laughter stays in the dark in the mirror's depths
to interrogate the pink bedroom
from within the next man's voice
interrogating your woman
asking her: where are you
where you were lost is where he enters

from the side where you have no complaints
in the place only a little higher than our heads
death continues its investment
all generations are so invested
to respond to the anxiety of the nighttime wilderness:

where are you

(2006)

Cupping Moonlight Through
a Crack in the Door

从门缝掬接月光

the seen not known, the seen not seen
no thing the soul, centered the center soars

held in these hands
the palms are written over with words unknown

the snow-covered ancestors have been received indoors

(2006)

This Word Thought

思这词

this thought, this unfillable
this meaning, this possessed mineral deposit
this power from the coal bed
penetrating into the blood stratum of the earth's layers
from the place of convergence from which people are isolated
holding only left hands, only ditches left over
think this death, without knowing how to die

an upright spine buried in sand
construction site cemetery, all on their shoulders
in the workers' shed, death is overexposed
the buriers release force
into the pit's past, faith thrown into time
the center is the before-death
the event, a sluice inside silence
on constructed ground, a newly built wilderness
bearing history, but no people
and in its safety
no motivation for us
to gaze at it, and while gazing
to be partially paid back

this, this is the collective pledge of suburban weeds

(2007)

On Dementia Mountain

痴呆山上

into the rain, raindrops
and the rain-dropping sky like a chime stone

a man leads a dairy goat
squats on the rock, a sort of loneliness

and in it, when there's nature to console a man
that distinctive desolation

when the mining region hides in gentle thunder
an early morning crevice

surveys a man
pure mass in silent shadow

the ancient town that buried ancient boats and ancient mirrors
has buried your hometown, too

good, that's how the ancient grave faces the scene from the hill
good, evil and its hunger are still so young

(2007)

Another Phase in Age
年龄中的又一程

exchanging our memories
needs our questions to breathe
knees rumbling
a spasm of the delivery line
sent to you, sent back from another

exchanging our silence
grass catches grass, no core at its depths
originally a blank, in tree sap
building its winter
from a coldness that had gone under review
speechless, soundless, and extraneous

the drumbeat is invariable
the monologue is an aside
in the relay of transforming into stone
the slight weight of seed
takes on a full-time darkness
in the collected works of pain
you are collected, we are harvested
you are separated anew, we are quarantined
the bulk future
runs again toward illiterate fear—

(2007)

Grass — Headwaters
青草—源头

hear the copper pain in our voices
leave behind the shape of a valley

what in life
buries the golden ear of wide-open hearing

what walks out
and tells the cruel world of the cliff of dripping tears

what is human, and what for the human
intervening in the vagrant landscape

(2007)

Come from Two Prisons

从两座监狱来

accumulate our lingering, outside struggle
the land the measuring implement of our behavior
occasionally recognizes freedom:

stones pushed to the summit
are sadly at their lowest level

within this lowness
through our inverted labors
toward a lower place drifts man

with a stalling field, living in excess
and in dread of what he's lived through
distance is only the outcome of measurement

beyond this report
little life is life

(2007)

To Have the Honor of Reading Shivers in the Moonlight

捧读月光下的颤栗

silently reading the evergreen's reflections
a former temple's broken roof tiles are in your hand
answering the wind that summons ten thousand trees

moonlight exhales a breath of stone
shutting white lotus enlightenment
zither sounds come, zither sounds go

sūtra rivers reciting words of inaction
the departed are the audience
the audience is silence

on this earth of insect chirps and quiet grasses
stele-shaped faces move without sound
testament to the forest having once been shadows of trees

people with hair untied rushing through an orphic wilderness

(2007)

Toward the Borges Bookshop
通往博尔赫斯书店

living streets, your address
is a city breakers flow through
only rejecting what has departed
when these restaurants, teahouses, select
another crowd, another death, another . . .

myth never regenerates
time overflows from a bowl it seems to have met
before, teaching passersby
not to look at dirty water, but to notice tragedy:
every going in is a going astray
and other than going astray, there will be no going in

the road scents these, so widens

(2008)

The Statue of the Reading Girl
读书的女雕像

read my thoughts as well
they're in — keeping us apart
when the thinker only thinks about action
but cannot capture the shadow of the bird in flight

lilac blinked an eye
your feet were sticking out of stone, silently
just then I heard music
ten toes digging into sand
fell and rose like piano keys

presence takes recruitment and staying
and leaves it where you are
absence — it's always
fully parallel with thought

so I advance
behind me, the eyes of a youth delivering flowers
are already wide open in fear

(2008)

Dead Desert Poplar Grove,
the Model Grove of Mourning
死胡杨林,哀悼的示范林

the baritone voice of the earth is done speaking its echo
a quiet representative, with what the water flows
and knows, having investigated too many hearts,
just makes the flow a testimony
light gushes toward us, as if shattered

in the mourners' old place
the stronger is the departed
and depth the point of pain
all force endures itself
where language is still located
wanting us to make of covered faces song

singing, we flow back, flowing into
that primordial chaos and the chaos beginning again
only in this spot of singing
is no protracted hell
only in singing this spot
does the cemetery start to resemble steps
from this absent present
from the place of our most fundamental pain
let us walk out, walk out anew —

(2009)

An Elegy for Mengmeng
献给萌萌的挽歌

1

discerning the shadow of classical dusk in the graveyard of poetry
facing you, that warm row
of the sea rushes its instantaneous
frontrunners, going back to antiquity
the last sound in a year
coming from a ground shaped like a mask

for that possible dialogue

all that's left of the statue of the choir is shoulders
pallbearers in the clouds walk past the summit
our grieving national forest stands within measurement
sharing the ideal country's long-gone ashes
a nation's stele forest knocking us back
listen to the loud self-criticisms of the passage of time

when you are singing out the location of silence

2

in this chorus-like moment of silence
the distant city sinks into punctuation
plus the dog-walker's overcast face
minus the building stone in the tragedian's hand
our great petrified forest introspects at full force

the whole symphonic movement is empty

lonesomeness is already a wall around the home
there are no other materials
to wait is to read through a book
the final pages are empty
the lonely white sky molds a cast
the first pages have not been turned to
a slab of marble staring at the poets

near those dressed in black they pluck your star-shaped heart

3
when in the dream what is upright, that forest of steles
gazes at the other place
in the strong music's moment of silence

thought is already such a long midnight
silence is already another kind of collection
discussion already another kind of wind another kind of rain
the past, surging yet still
turns again into a place of nobody, but of whispers

back then, the moment of silence was memory's
rhythm, grammar, logic
expanded into the whole pattern of our geography
and will not elapse without passing through words
evening prayers for the ancestors start again

your name begins its outward enunciation

4
in adequate language exchanging our silence
low whispers in low-air pressure lowlands
return to us the quietude of their original dwellings

those lodgings that rhetoric abandoned

this moment is memory, this moment forgetting

the one who left the road is already home
lead sunk in the lotus pond
the guard stands in a darkness
from which a day's worth of light has gone out
sisters' faces greeting gravel
to see how dahlias might make it over the wall
increase talent for speechlessness
and so reject the more eloquent passing by

the vacant space before your door is even more hollow

5
from a place never brought
send back the long-ago moment of silence
let the echoes of ratcheting weaken then strengthen
to wait is several words already
this life of ours, it's already the same evening

back then, quietude was a display:
in quietude, distance is shortest

we link
sisters — advancing white birches

in this quake felt midway through life
our shock is its strength
it knows when the end begins

you leave to keep it

6

from the concerted waiting of this silence
aphasia is full, abundant
this possession of absence possesses a face
bearing our beginning
and the other meadow that it's extended

the clock face happens to reveal half the east

another reading has begun
read the transformation that consumes
the motionless, and be more definite
depth still surges there

pour it full, then jump in

in the place that fits silence best
in that square stillness constructed for love

at the window where you have the west wind to yourself

7

in this land obstructed by magnified clarity
carry the gauged light into the room
the breath of the thinker is still here

midnight is already a moment without neighbors
speechlessness completes what it comprehends
aphasia is inaction's fiercest expression
back then, the sight of the mother was far, was deep

in that time most imbued with life
spacious, like a child's memory

home, so broad, like the last gate
as far as the eye could see, meditators who could no longer move
and you, measuring another kind of breath beyond must

at that time, stillness struck a deafening quake
in that place, you had already been heard

8
so let's be silent like this again
the heart is already another kind of weather
all heights are equal
all arrivers have submerged the terminus

ceaseless is its pinnacle

which is for a source
the initial recognition and repeated writing
in the silence that can accommodate its vastness
language trades away breath
vanishing vanishes into its memory

the far-off here

in the orchestrated calm
constantly rising, continually giving

emptiness at full sail drums up all the expressions of the departed

(2009)

The Passing of the Big Snake
大蛇的消逝

1

I am staring at a polyphonic flowchart before the table

like gravity, the *yin* river
runs through brother-shaped stones
a continually recovering psychology, a continual flow out of the
    plains
dipped full of pen ink, string and reed conjoined or in separation

a glance at the coarse braid dragging through the wheat field

a certain pain, which will proliferate from bronze
in the hermit's silence
focused toward the infinite: a crevice in concentration

desolate avenue, a crowd in period costume
bringing the underworld's black and white sky
parallel to a ladder-shaped lightning bolt, received as if bent at
    the waist
once dead die again, for that leap

on the great wind stele, expression is time

2

I keep staring at these black brush marks
the low frequencies released by the flowchart's low levels
cut through the inscription's surface clamor
and the quietude of its crevice depths

to leave this great doubt inside this great stillness

when wordlessness and rootlessness, both here and elsewhere
as in any mirror that can accommodate a river
the heart does not know itself

so in a room, I feel the speed of wind

and rush to stand, go look at the stars
these texts of life's commitment
how to make the whole landscape ultimately invisible
when the children in the melancholy hall
point at the statue, point at you

3
in this other zone between intuition and exegesis

an echo-storing head, your head
has long been used to spasms of the helmet
no brain inside, or else only brain
one time, nothingness had weighed enough weight

shrinking could be limitless, too

in this wild zone between blood and book
you don't look at me, but know me
where rantings contentedly converge
you know my kind
at the spot that miracles seem to smudge

the stick of humanity is brandished

to lure the necks of riddles camouflaged in multicolor to
    straighten
and voice their most accusatory sigh:
other than myth, all is fiction

history like the moment the rug is rolled up

4
an incomparable oral cavity opens

an apple-shaped evil rolls along your face
while ripping up your head
a strange laugh turns into a grimace
as if contorted by synthesis
to adapt to the tyranny of logic:

one's last words must be silent

a bridge bows, an omen
crushing odd words, shadows bigger than the temple
and you, entangled on a child's wagon
and then hung from it, hanging
that thing that exists beyond form
a wisp of green smoke, threads of clues

what's smelled is only breath
a living being in the form of fog disperses
marriage's first alliance in chaotic grassland's depths

criticism will have no further scrolls

5
light and its raft row into the distance in the picture

youths walk by, one after the other, to be returned to
flood, cliff wall, yesterday's face
like this geology, lot in life, fragmentary writing
leaving only jotted-down wriggles

at that time, I heard the jungle singing accompaniment
lighter even than the sigh of a snake
I believe you still sift through the depths of the institute
from its acute angles, its dimensions
the point it does not broker
the lotus pond, like a one-eyed star
peeking at a sea of clouds on the other side of tragedy

moonlight like the first waters, the final waters

fluid excerpts, as of melodies
still being strummed, melding into the scenery
disclosure corresponding to fastening
so as to conform to your arrival

and then, blocked from restoration to the original state

(2009)

Stored in Words
存于词里

to leave in dust, as where bones are buried
is no one, words reject no words
abandon words, measure echoes:

the stress field of one's lot

from a gone forever that flows
growing into the timeless
timeless and perpetual
no words in common

we have no, they have no
no other allegory

(2010)

In Its Within
在它以内

bury your words and take your death
and add it in
so minuscule it's no longer a seed

life in a bowl
is uneven, yet waveless

so humanity's boundaryless expectations
are like permutated gravestones
making their way through an entire nation

(2010)

Drinking Blood in the Wordless Zone
在无词地带喝血

say what history does not say
this unheard, without forehead

this silence of many vocal parts
choral wordlessness
life being what's sung

wordless, speechless, boundless

words being what's said, words'
remnants, saying everything

(2010)

Walking Out from a Book
从一本书里走出来

the miner's eyes brighten like oil lamps
there is no other depth
in the abyss words shine outward:
in the place of mourning, no depth
all lights in the cherry orchard light up
the people there, stacked evenly each by each

in the place they have always been
climbing from its mouth
the dead begin to breathe:
the depth, it is ours . . .

with them sleeping on you, you're able to rewrite

(2010)

No Answer from the Depths

深处没有回答

depths bury the valley
when the handcart pushes away blood clots
the word foundry it carries
is theirs, is them

this moment this is at the guarded home

time is not here, but amid permission
waiting for these words to be dug up
to be preserved, above all to be begun
this regrettable lifelong term
this stele forest in back of all that lives

(2010)

Cemetery in the North
北方的墓地

on the road we come and go on
carrying our ancestors' dust, listen
to the homeland drums in a faraway place
fear invades the better years from inception

we do not know why thunder peals

thought holds up the stone man's head
the boatman defends the instep's veins
all that is complete the river has carried away
to wherever it can burst through dikes, to where dams intervene

cemeteries in the north swell like the tide

at the time of the recitation of floods
gaze down on our sail-like words
silently reading what no longer stirs our hearts
but which still beats to their beat

forgetting is the same river
in this dusk down a path
going with what the water patches up, what it takes away
the drummer searching for a source along the paradigmatic axle
is still impacted by the force of flowing into stone

look for the hidden mileage between taken-down wheels

(2010)

Recollection of the Black-White Forest

追忆黑白森林

black tree white tree, only white candle all night —
night all day, white candle equal height to trees
black words bleed, overturning the grass of the living
red flower white flower, laying out a home that can be questioned
words seep out of words, white temple white tiles white pagoda
    white horse
song murders nightingale, sword executes white flower

from the end of these names, crumbling wall bloody wall
looking toward us, a trace of blood a trace of word, coming
    toward us
blood is not water, water is not water
meeting redundant people, people who will be reseen

(2010)

The Soundless Road
无声的道路

following the cloud, homeless like a cloud
looking for a place for words to live, from
the sky, this explosion-like bright mirror
ebb tide–like stone wall, an entity connected head to head
still has pent-up impasses of pen and ink

words appear on their stern flank no more
on it or within it, it is all that it is
so that they may already be fated
to experience the place of their own emptiness

when the known does not see
the seen is unknown
recognition without encounters
no records is called testimony

thought will not be tightly knit in the forest
the rage of thunder knows not where it comes from
what's falling now is rain, rain
in a moment of catching silence in cupped hands
sitting as ever before the table
the seeker has forgotten himself
but cannot give this stillness to anyone else

perhaps that's nothing but the road's feeling of limitlessness

(2010)

Memorializing These Grasses
纪念这些草

secrets write the grass in our voices
grass carries on grass, grass read aloud by silence
beneath grass, a kneeling formation
that has never petrified

at the depths of sorrow the grass, since it
preserves people vanished
in the depths of names, will flash
the light of conjunction in the radiant forest

the depths will not close again
but only accept grass's cover

every word comes from here

(2010)

They Hold Hands Underground As Well

他们在地下也手拉手

at the deepest point of burial
take the month and its vestiges
make no sound, but quickly reveal their sky

when they do not die, bring their deaths
and walk away from the people run aground
they never became skeletons
never were loyal to death

death without limit is no longer death

(2011)

In the Silent Valley Is Buried the Moving
沉默的山谷里埋着行动者

the plateau between two hopes
is made wordless again by renovation
some still weep, but are not crying
the weight of the dead is lightened
to certify this wordlessness

there are no lambs in an age of silence
so pigeons fly out of blood nests
the world in the eulogy
recedes from the human trace
the midwife's wavering still casts a shadow
so the discussion in the umbilical cord can continue

fate is in this speaking out—

(2011)

Reading Great Poems
读伟大诗篇

this standoff between fairy tale and myth
desolation always comes before illumination
apexes always cave in with perfection
gravestones see the farthest

all low points were apexes once

from the abyss that can understand
echoes only the silence of the other
heights are still low points
love at the lowest point

let the dialogue between thought and silence continue

(2011)

Father

父亲

standing in this brightening light waving
wishing I won't ever dream of him again

but I'm always looking at that big hill
as tranquil as a mandible dragged off by a horse
speaking in a whisper
to shoo away flies from the faces of the dead
I've never been so afraid
I know, as soon as the sun rises
these faces will darken
I don't dare be afraid

from the length of a stretch of rope
infinite starlight gallops far
father, you have detached from here
I'm still wearing the mask of a horse
by the riverside, drinking blood . . .

father, nightmares are dreams
father, nightmares are not dreams

(2011)

Borges
博尔赫斯

before every prophet's grave stands a crowd of the deaf
they cannot get by him
as if in closing in on itself
after the din is just more din
everyone: dreamless
while he is our symptom
in the face of a packed-in blank space, an enigma
and its intense four walls
long ago his death passed through a narrower crevice:
the sea is not a large quantity of water
it is a crowd swallowing a person
he is eyeless, but he is our vision

(2011)

In Front of the Silent One I'm Drinking Water
我在沉默者面前喝水

I drink the lightest, a sentence
a phase of life, not belonging

not shouting, neither whispering
I am at the lowest point

nudging words, and so nudge
and possess an expansive lot in life

pots large and small hold the sound of rain
and drink down my silence

I kneel in an inadvertent place
where no one is, unashamed

being with no one is its own defense

(2011)

From Golden Ears
That Might Have Heard Silence
从可能听到寂静的金耳朵

green grass — withered grass
two words

looking over a nest of weeds
mother's five copper toes

all my words
pressed here, all my homes

converging right here

(2011)

The Wind Blowing In from Somewhere Spacious

从空阔处吹来的风

inspired on occasion, on occasion numb
that bit of always blurry sky

no one twisting their faces toward anyone
from the part where the landscape cannot speak

the girl's tears, held in the boy's hand
rivers, rolling outside poems

an infinite endpoint
that faraway here

as if it were White Sands Gate

(2011)

Greeting the Words
That Burst Through the Forehead
迎额头崩出的字

slow, no match for the moment
succinct, would be better soundless

exquisite, thus omitting
abstracted, thus transmitted

(2011)

The Cemetery Is Still Accepting Members
墓园仍在接纳

the travelers have long been stationed
love and no love, buried face to face

the moment of silence not yet onstage
the dead are still waiting

the watches on their wrists still going
love is without a grave

the overseer reads a larger map

(2011)

The Shang Yang Exhibit
尚扬画展

calligraphy is a matter of mind
the way a word is the memory of line
a painting is silent, hiding inside its substance
from pain, that shaped spirit
the severed nerve is made to move
once seeming human-shaped, seemingly once known
don't tell us who they are
excessively clear is only dust

(2012)

Arrival

到来

toward the blackening roof ridge
see what it is that looks both like a light and an eye
beneath the eaves, a jug of water has been filled
the weather leapt over the wall
the air didn't vibrate
as if it had come purely from time
this squeezing of time
is a moment that was not foretold

in a sufficient silence
with things that must blacken
there was no story behind the door
I did not peek
flowers were blooming rapidly

the ten thousand things did not evade it

(2012)

The Landscape of Terms Is Not for Viewing
词语风景, 不为观看

a field of leaves pressing on the chest can, if forced, become a
    world
for a breath of pure air
but too pure, and it's like an earthly crime

the full scene doesn't do anything, no morning sunshine where
    it's clear
the world doesn't speak of itself, that's the scatter of stars
everything turns trivial, but freedom is not trivial
extracting what's richest from language
to provide children with things caught after nightfall

lonesomeness is grain, you cannot not be there
when expensive paper leaves no trace
no words on it, no you
only what cannot be erased can be new
only what's most real is worth burying

after death, it's probably still like this
destruction knows no exhaustion, they
are already using copper to cast you
consolation jolts awake, inside generation
the baby next door is about to start crying again

(2012)

Talking the Whole Way

一路接说

at the age above the snow line
the wind that enjoys silence, abundance, and wordlessness
will not learn to read for a blind landscape
strum the tree that can grow golden fingers
behind you, words knot their own chain
may emptiness harvest good wheat
there's a limit to water, but not to fluidity
a drop of water that keeps expanding
walking along, arms swinging, and the lotus pond swells

that's the way you walk to your backwater
in late periods, no requests
just gaze at women, they
won't come in, but nakedly face the green hills
while you, you stay in their reproduction
in the head's obstruction, what's hard to forget
is the horse herd, still crossing the waters
in a stronger beat
one heart, the myriad things overlap
no line pulled in the hand, the instant can still be sent far away

disappearance is but reclusion's other dance

(2012)

Ten Pencils Clipped on an Ear
耳朵上别着十支铅笔

still embracing the wind, but unable to keep up with fallen leaves
why are you still here
peeking at what you had
why would you leave it

life eats the eternal
why answer it, when words eat words
even the wellspring conserves
this is the sunset in your room

but dim light is still light
a fracture, a core matter
that by chance leaves a few words: don't do anything
once asleep, you are the wind

what's still waiting, then missed
is the horizon persisting
life counters the effortless
or else death, there are other contents

write it, then forget it
you and not your residue
have an answer deep down
after death is just afterward

but you're still too young, not yet the clouds

(2012)

Words as Grain, Asleep in the Gospels
词如谷粒, 睡在福音里

what's awaited is never punctual
stern fruit in formation on the bookshelf
is order not knowing the way
only dice can make it through the calendar

in freedom is nothing
no other quality on earth
once metal has eaten enough plums
only the breath of stationery is left in the room

along words' axle, the core's veneration
dream and knowledge come from the same library
for load bearing, not for sealing
waiting is just reading all the way through

outside words, inside the jumble
exhausted, waking at earliest
dawn light, only seven cockcrow
abstract gesticulations are fit to grab this hour

writing is what makes antiquity endurable —

(2012)

Stars Like Human Eyes,
Humans Like Oil Lamps

星如人眼, 人如灯盏

beyond the door is the thousand-year sleeper
the heart cannot hold a century
when the blacksmith's body twists
he can see today —

confusion is still in the furnace
no forging images for totems
the meditator's head hangs toward the furnace
no covering of faces for homelands
maxims only meld with fire
but the fallow can pass through the needle's eye

back to the door of memory, unplanned yet certain
there is still great mourning, without great wings
wordless, silent only to differentiate
but without words, so without waves

wherever we go, cuckoos all around

(2012)

Taking Fire from Song
从歌内取火

the ultimate and the *en route*
cast shadows that used to unite us
as still as a valley burying a kettle

silence has buried the conversers
longing is ruined by a seal
the faraway no longer equals mileage
some infinitely distant rumbling
approaches the low moan of the road:

there's no way to save what the tomb does not have

with no antiquity, there's no resonance
outside the pit, no conscience
in the mausoleum in which fangs are buried
rust drips off the statue's fragmentary nose
down an edge that can die without limit

against a grieving earth the deepest parents
hold candles for the asphyxiated sky
death speaks loudly through ten thousand candles
blood couldn't flow as a higher form
but today will conclude after tomorrow
the graveyard comes as surging breakers

until the unapologetic earth's funereal face is slowly unrolled

(2012)

At the Exit You Say: Entrance
你在出口说：入口

a leaf bigger than a heart
but its core is not there

every word is not itself
they will not turn into banners

still where the grindstone rolls
guarding sand and wings

still under the grindstone
using separation to make soil

you join in
with the beloved, face to face

your blood, reincarnated no more
grass beginning to resemble wheat

you are more and more yourself

(2012)

Listening to the Mother Grove's Chorus Behind the Father Grove

听父亲林后面母亲林的合唱

under the sand, age protrudes
erases what's written, past
unfolding in the grass, erases what's rewritten
that's how the river inscribes, how it flows
erasing what's endlessly rewritten

from the refracted mileage of these words
the heart is land reserved
the dead — the consoler
who once here intoned:
what's to be dug is the crane, make it stay

to keep calling to the man hauling water across the river

(2012)

Waiting for the Raging Dust to Fall

等激荡的尘埃落下

dead rose valley still bears the hoofprints of untamed horses
I don't mean horses, but horse piss
the *pow* it reports trickling down horse legs
the sky that makes dreams stay, deep enough to seem like a pit

sculptures pass like wind and storm clouds

replacing candles and spirits in jail
it's power that makes pain, pain that makes people
from here, zither music can establish boundaries
the Russian coast juts forward, winding around your silhouette
I don't mean the homeland

all it chases is death's final farewell

(2012)

To Face the Sea for Long Is to Face Forgetting

长久地对着大海，就是对着遗忘

the stone man's sturdy neck mixes with boat-mooring iron piles
hands behind her back the ice skater on the clock face chases the
    hour hands
only five p.m., and the sailor is standing in his piss
the east is read through, the portrait of a giant
looking more like his descendants each time

people who say the end of dry land can only be the sea are wrong
no one who only knows the map will ever make it there

the sea is nothing but the navigator's log

(2012)

If a Flaw Were a Sin

如果缺陷是罪

watching others suffer sin is a sin
you look in the mirror, which only reflects their faces
bitterness eats you, but also eats them
a look into the bowl is a look into their immortality

(2012)

Explode, Bloom

爆炸, 开花

open the flowers that can hurt
the catastrophe is your timbre
let daggers bloom

blooming from this, this overflows
unknown light finds a finer sheath
from within this paralyzed curse

the sword is split
in the scenery, in its scenery
from this already past as yet

desolate textbooks, infant like a lamp
far-off home
already a stone, already

words that can hurt will not be pursued

(2012)

From a Show of Magnificent Gratitude
从一场盛大的感谢

the setting sun occupies the avenue
silence has become a veranda from which all is viewed
on the planes upon which clouds construct their gradual odd
    vistas
the elders still glow, they just no longer shine
youth has become the sunset clouds in the statue's eyes

on the line where the myriad things leave their shadows
to plummet and to ascend are equally grand
thanks to the remuneration of things
from the disbanded gift
is spit one last brick of gold

reality's sun returns to a carnivorous sea

allegorizing affection for the setting sun

(2012)

No Home in Words
词内无家

no name, no grave, no home
the nameless sung by the nameless

and add to that no sound
silent, but loud

the sky opens awhile

waves at the depths of deep silence
swelling already

rise up to yourself

(2012)

A Fine Breeze Comes

好风来

coming has already followed away
it comes and goes for ignorance

what a flowing as of water
has taken, has filled in

what a performance as of wind
has lyricized and laid out

the dead endow themselves into the ringing of chimes
a fine breeze, a fine disappearance

a fine breeze coming

(2012)

Sobbing at Midnight

夜半哭声

the woman's sobbing was a ripping at first
and continued into a sluice as of melody
lotus pond water swelling at one side
the man used low-voice theory
but the sobs could not be stifled
the lotus pond is chipping like a basin
the lower his voice, the louder the sobbing

I had stopped work early, and wasn't listening intently
but couldn't stand the silence any longer
I opened the window, a young couple's shadows

walking toward the starting point of humanity

(2012)

If Dreaming Were Something for Another
如果做梦是他人的事

then it would always be unclothed, but never exposed
where dreams are most spacious
your reader wears your mask
you hide

as style is like a birthmark
words leak everything
you are silent

your silence is starting to help another

(2012)

No Dialogue Before Writing
书写前没有对话

the early morning does not answer the crop field of logical
    thought
the income of dreams is not the income of movement
don't store the sea in stories
the more speech, the less drama
freedom, a pool of sonorous water
this clear, and thus verbose:
you must possess, but must say no

that's how metaphor's water level rises so high

from the broad genre of vindication
all surplus originates in lack
in human nature, there is no mileage
in health, no life
endlessness is not enough illusion
taking shape only when you're absent

but emptiness does not fear the myriad things

go circulate all that has never been dormant

(2013)

Speechless Between Partners
对象间无语

before meeting, no expression
at the tear, still no reveal
too late, and yet too early
the forest is like fog

words, in a place very far away
are equivalent, but do not meet
the attainment of meaning makes them transform
lightning grabs the picture
dark and still, getting vehement
disintegrated, but still not released

to keep a silent cutting edge

(2013)

A Desk Has No Edge

一张书桌没有边缘

the horizon is never whole
tracking is futile
the dream is the ignorance of the dreamer

from this incomprehensible field
nothing can be called death, and life is not disclosed
yet anxious to be dreamt
this is the road
to destroy it, understand it
this is rhythm
let the dream interpreter enter dreams
the dream is the land
keep the grain of your personality
to prolong it, let it go fallow
light can be late

the line of the poem has not retreated

(2013)

Starlight So Limpid

星光如此清澈

limpid enough to stir the scenery in the head
this beneficial stillness, stillness of beneficence
transmitted to the sound of mystery's every corner
held because vast, hidden because held
and so greeting the modesty between beams of light

because it remembers the starry sky, the heart begins winter's
    performance
inside a small opportunity, stirring it
—this strenuous resonance

what wants to be said is crying
what cannot be said is language

this is what we live for, O lord

(2013)

The Secret of Eating Almonds

吃杏仁的秘密

living's meaning, a kind of death
in front of a temporary birth

you are its gift
siding only with it

to die seizing death's consent
toward hope's layers of parents

a sort of unfinished death
children who want to love grass only belong to grass

you are each of them, walking to the next
no further

with no significance, no ashes
death only speaks in a strange land

the echo insists that it belong to eternity, just for once

(2013)

The Monitor from the Cloud Layer
从来自云层的监听

from this omnipresence
silently reading humanity

maintaining that fake eye
in the green desert

unlimited surplus
less than it oversees

from this nowhere — this is somewhere
on the horizon of human physics

maintaining human matter
another world inside a shut mouth

the horizon still someplace above

(2013)

In So Far a Place
在多远的地方

how long keeping to how far
keeping to human wilderness
that belongs just to humans

blind in so far a place
these godless seconds
this fruitless wordlessness
finding its object of prayer

only in your eyes sings
this land of promise

(2013)

Sing an Unsingable Song

唱唱不下去的歌

sing the unconcluded heart
from this cause coming over the mountains

sing the vast parents behind the clouds
what's gone and won't return has nourished you

when what floats leads what upholds what floats
now bright and light, now somber and quiet

sing out what must be gone through:
both people and landscape

separated by nothing, nowhere not connecting

(2013)

Listening to the Rain
Is Nothing Like Watching the Rain
听雨不如观雨

these raindrops that are about to speak but stop
leave brush marks inactive and indolent

writing from the stratosphere
it bears words, born from it

where words are, home is
groundwork in cloud

may comprehension come leisurely
cloud to be left on the table

no peaks, only summits

(2013)

From an Unfamiliar Forest
从一片陌生的林

what is hidden within each species
seems able to hide
rejecting the blank
to squeeze in exchange

from the verso of a leaf
we introduce each other
only with life's core
arranging the unenunciated

these trees will sway in words
speaking with what's yet to arrive

(2014)

May You Be Happy

祝你快乐

I am in your forgetting
but my flower is your flower
I'm not searching, I've
cracked open your dreams
and started living inside them

goodbye — uncertain
flowers only bloom on performers' fingertips

may you miss me

(2014)

See What the Plains See
看原野所看的

on a great slope both
like a mausoleum and a cannon tower
the sun's blood forest moves on
no vestiges at the tip
forgetting ascends the throne again

that is where we were cast off
in a silence that has always been quiet
material and burden together
do not equal a mineral vein
a road leads to a visit
without revealing language's trace

we begin to hear our own voices:
rebuilding its surface

(2014)

From the Abyss That Can Understand
从能够听懂的深渊

thunderstorm and lightning didn't clarify one word
debating about the north wind of each
in the strenuousness of recasting lightning
the sky permits wordlessness, and also song
sung back from the precipice

when history was most taciturn
the howls of the world passed through false mouths

the world is a show of protracted lightning

(2014)

Just a Few Books
只有几本书

and the echo, only on the major scale
resounding the endless and the timeless
the candle's half-diminished scale descends where it must
the wordless and the breach
begin to be parallel

we didn't understand
what music was

through the odd noises of word groupings
a few books rise
in the convection of the word's linked prayers
let be become be

we are still in the clamor and roar
chasing your silence

(2014)

See the Smoke in the Bottle, the Sail in the Bottle

看瓶子里的烟，瓶子里的帆

the idea is like a boat sliding by
read pearls, beginning to roll
internal cries of cliffs beginning to resemble the sea

in the bottle of a concept
stern faces move along one by one
rowed by many oars

Picasso's fingers all wear prison uniforms
to paint an emptiness a huge hand knit
the head tied to the mast was the first to see it

the front disappears
in the bottle it's uncommonly quiet, as in the sand
the key remains curious about the tides

birds call to the earth, knowing only the waves

(2014)

Into the Room
入屋

but where is the room
with no ultimate, no need to look

light answers loudly
behind the door, no world

nobody inside
at the end, nothing

no thing, so some bottom
the door must stay open

to enter again, but not to live there

(2014)

At a Point We Call *En Route*
在我们称之为途中的一点

dream and sigh have melted into one
clamor and silence cannot return to legend
where there is great terminology, there will be a great repose
ore's ancient stupor still groaning

guard what must be, and what cannot
sleep and wakefulness are always together
never ending, as never begun
turning your face to me, you

   turn millennia

(2014)

The Force of Forging Words
铸词之力

outside force, continuing on
from enough, is insufficient hallucination

light vanishes with feathers
stillness cannot be forfended

candles stuck with wings know only to advance
what's most loved is dark and quiet

this is rationale's wasteland
but the ethics of poetry

dream and the boat on the shore must join forces
if words can spill beyond their own bounds

only there, to test the hearing of the end

(2014)

Neither

两者

in love is no school
neither a way to wither into understanding
nor to stock up significance
love cannot realize reduction
even less does it know what's redundant

and such is the burden
such heaviness, yet without weight
the end, though not stopping in death
it brokers no fiction
but narrates only this lack

neither has qualms about all that is

(2014)

A Kind of Green Once Came to the Door
某种绿曾至家门

once stars, once windows
stone elders still remember silent readings at the edge of the
    woods
once there, still there

at the portico where life and death both vanish
still led by the immortal arms of the elders
is left a home that can be questioned

still writing indefatigably in the expansive meadow
our sod roof still green
we are lonely as poplars planted by our great-grandfathers

our loneliness, it is built of flesh

(2014)

The Road Is Not Set for the Seeker
路不为寻找者而设

until meeting what you believe
there is no arrival

your road has widened
a tidewater of travelers splits off a moment

there's no road, it's all road

(2014)

Chama River, Spectral Pasture
查马河, 幽灵牧场

from the picture, a river punctures the heart of the past
when stoneware and cloud rolled together
cracking open the dark red throat of the valley

swords divided good and evil
sheep devoured their shepherds
history was peaceful, but fearsome

along the spiritual contour line
clouds hide spears and shields
that yet meet this vertical river

nature is not troubled by depletion
those dwarves are coming back again
to unite with the limitless patience of the sky

(2014)

Lamp Against Candle

灯紧挨着烛

in the lamp it's all ideas
outside sleep
 outside waking
between here and not here

in the head the lamp shines
erase implication
you pull yourself up on the lamp's shadow
and leap for a more human-shaped place

wholly parallel with writing

(2015)

The Waves Released to the Zither

随琴声释放的波浪

telling time for the tides
season and sequence are no longer together
spring and autumn equinoxes snuggle
cellos grow oars

sails spread their wings, sticking out from the fleet
torpedoes yearn to open their own rivets
a caress-like calm catches up with
the explosion, which startles nothing anymore
birds begin to chase bullets
that's how words arrive

from the upside-down reflections of this lovely earth

(2015)

Dear Light Dances By

亲爱的光舞蹈着走过去

the stage is overgrown with grass
I have only a pair of baby hands
still digging in the depths

that you, my you
both are one

the valley is silent
a pair of jaguars
have our faces

a family walks by
I cannot follow them

cloud's sisters walking on the field ridge

a woman already in the moonlight
laughing pearls, raging pearls
line up anew around her neck

each pearl is screaming:
loneliness is the biggest rose

(2015)

A Round Sung Between Eyesight and Eyesight
从这目光与目光的轮唱

I only see your crystal body
in it, there's a pair of goldfish

our infinite yesterday
guarded over, looked after

by the icebergs — multimillion-year-old brides
together already with happy dreamlessness

from a round sung by eyesight and starlight

crystal crackles
another season on the lawn of our lives

already together with the unmoving dancer
emerging from the choral twilight afterglow

the theater is sawed open
so treat it like a heart

I'm still consoling the goldfish
a smashed zither still playing:

I am your mother

(2015)

The World in Words   One Oar, One Wave
词间人世   一桨, 一浪

stabilize breathing the rippling surface
all generations' sail corners unfurl

    stele forest on paper, the compass of stillness

touching indefinite scale
paying balance's specifications

    perilous tower willow, solitary constellations

in a flash arrives no blame
in a strike not early or late

    a ship in driving rain, the human heart in dark of night

past the knife-cut water, the formless gate
raided, all between conclusions

(2015)

This Is a River Without Memory
这是一条没有记忆的河

let only what must go flow
if the river carries meaning, it can't stream away

give it the road
to catch up to the flow, this settling

stone starts singing lullabies
mother has become a mountain forest

from this site of no return
can be understood the river's narration

    belonging to returning

(2015)

No Stars in the Sky, No Lights on the Bridge
天上无星, 桥上无灯

a landscape painting walks to its own margins
shadows like smoke or spirits, still moving

like what's latent of a dream, a lute lies on its case
the hand that strums it, which had been cut off

jolted from headwaters, the previous guest
remains in the table's knife scratch, clearly visible

shattered eras want you to keep
playing for the contours of an aphasic world

elapsed apexes want the silent one in the teahouse
to interpret his own heart this way

the sound of former readings, pulling you
out of the mirror

whoever holds your hand holds onto
a river that no one has claimed

(2015)

No Other Depth
没有另外的深处

in the eulogist's old place
are only those pits

pits that are also bowls
the depth won't close again

the lowest level is not soil
not even burial

eulogy always looks ahead

(2015)

Hearing the Bleeding Melody in Your Voice
听你声音中流血的旋律

dancing milk room
reaches a safe place

where there is neither hatching
nor any furthered death

where it is not a region
and you are together

where once more it speaks here

(2015)

Light Coming from Before, Sing: Leave

从前来的光, 唱：离去

lightning head
that is your song
go back to a turbulent blue sky
you are another of its elations

live at stop
stopping where it's fullest

tomorrow's already past
already offered
the past is still unknown
already spoken

the limit belongs to you
nobody can have that name

(2016)

From the Other—A Crowd of Me

从他者——众我

invite yourself
from us, each of us

thinking back on someone, an other
in such a soliloquy

limited, hence you
hence us

hence the mourning of the tall silhouette

(2016)

Where Phrase Blooms
在词语的开花之地

the grass of passion decreases
on the basis of us, decreases

lessens, even less
less than to say

every leaf is applauding
more than the everyday

(2016)

Never Caught Up with Myself
从未跟上自己

I've walked past me
life has experienced me
a boy walks by
I chase him, screaming:

you're not you—

(2016)

If No Echo, No Monologue

没有应和就没有独白

wordless, but not quite silent
unless to say love, unless not to speak
— there is leftover gunpowder in this line
becoming a simplified beginning

poetry is a sky giving this its performance

(2017)

The Desire of the Rose Now the Same As the Desire of Swords
玫瑰的欲望已经与剑的欲望一致

That Time
那时

why does the camel need twin humps to make it through the
    desert?

I look at you, you only look at yourself
I look there, I only see you

I look at things I cannot see
I see time — that long, long rose

at that time the lion could still think, no flames of fury in the
    beauty's eyes
at that time we could still walk into things we could not
    understand

it's the heart that creates the invisible, between riddle
and its four walls, letting the parable of life pass through the ring

the way my sunlight might pierce your eyes
to see some even farther place

women's bodies used to be a meadow, still releasing all that
    dreams received
the river's flow is slowed by the breath of their bathing

at that time you appeared, planting your feet, to stop my pacing
love should have no name, to darken the hill that grows only
    roses

only two trees are left there, one the shadow of the other

trees have no heart, and stand straight because no one will
    embrace them
but taller still when leaned on by sterilized women

a woman's statue in a corner of the park, everyone walking by
tosses a coin into her mouth
at that time I heard a kind of sound, softer than a snake's sigh

beauty kneeling there, as if for some first offense
as stable as creation

that's how the snake listened to my tale
vines sprouting wings entwining around the clock, too little for
    love to use

in silence is a never-ignited lamp, light it
to illuminate each day that never reached us

not knowing what emotions want, the bird hides its head in
    implication
feed it with what wisdom is in the cage

you hide behind your smile, the sun telling lies inside your eye

I steal your words while you toss the salad
at what degree is guessing stealing?

your heart is hiding in back of whatever I'm looking for
in back is its entire location

the caged animal pricks up its ears, meatballs in the clouds, clouds
    full of fervor

on its own in the darkness, as are you, the sun secretly shines
we'll just have to stay silent with eyes open

your eyes are two windows open at sea bottom
the stars above our heads just a bunch of TVs

oyster shells are dumped onto the bed where we turn and
    overturn
I enter the other side of night

the fifth season is already singing falsetto

an apple smiles on the windowsill, the rose only knows growing
    thorns
all words brighten

tomorrow is in the clock already, a sixth toe starts growing on
    your foot

two great birds, featherless, bodies all muscle
in the dark we identify each other

honeysuckle hanging midair like a right hook
powerless to restrain its conclusion

the desire of the rose now the same as the desire of swords

a pair of shoes maintains the shape of your toes
the dancer walks by, meaning there'll be as many times turning
    back
as there are times setting out

I get near you, wait for you, my flowers
blooming on another's collar, I on your dust

I am your landscape painting flittering back and forth
I am your lover

I'm not me, but Jesus is about to leap from my heart
I am your downfall

count my glass tears, you already grasp the story of the future

from behind you're more complex than you are, I'm still
    observing
the field between us

lonesomeness is a lighthouse, parallel with love
sneering springs from self-mockery, via justification

the rose is gray, its shadow rose-colored

my face is half of my mask

no one is themselves, I see feather-shaped shadows fighting with
    the wind

witnesses help us forget

I insist on a state of being alive, my solitude brokers no
     disturbance

I'm a writer who rolls through seven bedsheets a year
I rely on nervousness more than I rely on your bed

I recollect in song, and rock the arrowheads on my back

whoever empathizes with pain, go count wool

and take away my drum, burying it is worth more than beating it

in back of me, these words use my voice
that's how strong the coffin is

loneliness is for the young
a woman whose eyelids are covered with dead moths takes aim at
     my constellation

fishers stare with fish eyes, observing their own hearts

trees see further, with no more obstructions, having given them
     all up
the children slapping trees are all angels, each shorter than the
     last

practice this imperfection, the earth has no other sight
the world has an aching mother

father blocked by mother, the cello has a pear-shaped posterior

I'm afraid of thunder, and so's mom; I love what I fear

a great bird is staring at me with a maternal expression
I cover my face, happily growing teeth

I'm wearing clothes a goldfish has worn, endlessly taking candy
    out of its pockets

the tree wears a boy's shorts wiping the sky
the letters sent to mother's grave have arrived

I dream, dreaming I'm no longer a horse

inaction is too expensive, the thunder of old age sent it
lightning loves that it never possessed it

the soul was unprepared, precious objects are in hiding
more faithful than mother's grave

gravestones kiss gravestones; between them the effort to open up
    flesh is renewed

a horse comes galloping over, we know each other, so the horse
    gallops away
another horse comes galloping, so we gallop away

Going to Samaria
去撒玛洛

nineteenth century still there drinking milk
the planter and the breeder both approach life
two rows of plant-shaped clubs being brandished
waving at the time we began
    going to Samaria

another evening in the rainbow
on things like boats and also like cars
the ice-seller pushes us into the ocean
where we came from

    going to Samaria

in another heart's November
daughters pluck stars from the ceiling of a wave
buoy-like little mothers push rain clouds to move on
an archipelago appears in the vegetable broth

    going to Samaria

dads suspended — on that big shark net
the past's dark sky walks by performing
the beautiful spouse's plastic claws
still grasping at my future lion face

    going to Samaria

From Where Light Rushes Out
从光芒的冲出处

I avoid entering your mouth like fire
occupy this nothing

when you're just blood, and blood is bloodthirsty
the earth has desire's deeper color

the oar is stuck into the river's abdomen
your voice diminuendos and crescendos

in the measure where the chimes still ring beehives
what's loved has no boundaries

the earth is naked, pain truly has a price
if love were free, return

to collect the years in the depths of light

Being Love's Neighbor
与爱为邻

your house is empty
a sword suspended
just to be sharpened on your body

you think of a woman
her feet as cold as a shoehorn
and just as in need of tenderness

the window opposite is wide open
a man is smacking
a butt that's stronger than a bathtub

you think of another man
he used to be you
you raise your hand

and wish the world a peaceful night

Wake
醒来

memory cracks in a room without mirrors
the window curtain keeps the lover's expression
you are walking away in a friend-like disaffection
love is a matter from another kind of prison

Unless Unsaid
除非不说

the rose only knows growing thorns
candles shapeshift in discourse

    unless no love

alcohol burns no more
silk bolts still on fire

    unless said

always saying goodbye
the first time without sorrow

Soliloquy
独白

the loved has no remainder
it does not love what it guards
but loves the fragmented

to make the soliloquy stronger—

My Heart
我的心

is where you sink and float
where you drift away
unable to say goodbye
separation is a sort of vow

embracing together
neglected together

be real, waves
have no terminus

so have only loneliness

Looking at You, I See Only There
我望着你, 只望到那里

on the other side of our common sky
there is no more of our standing beneath the starlight

no more, I'm afraid, no more
in the depths you say are there

how large the world
that has drowned this world

The Flower Blooms Like a Sail
花开得像帆

if the things drive by
our pasts the way they hope

the water surface carries our reflections
what follows water's flow is growing

so, the moment of happiness is the moment of memory
so, remembrance is pursuing what is ahead

so distant, now a blessing

(2018)

AMSTERDAM'S RIVER
(1989–2004)

Amsterdam's River

阿姆斯特丹的河流

in the November nightfall city
there is only Amsterdam's river

suddenly

the tangerines on my tree at home
shake in the autumn wind

I close the window, but no use
the river flows upstream, but no use
that sun inlaid with pearls, rising

no use
pigeons disperse like iron filings
and the streets with no boys suddenly seem so spacious

after autumn rain
the roof that's crawling with snails
— my country

slowly floats by, on Amsterdam's river

(1989)

Walking Toward Winter

走向冬天

the sound the leaves make changes
rotten cores, piercing the eyes of passers-by

on the rice-drying red roof of days past
glistening insect corpses pile up as autumn's contents

autumn is brushing wool overcoats preparing for winter
fungus makes its way toward winter out of dilapidated coffins

youth in the sunlight, turned ugly
marble parents wailing

when water passes under the well
the plow is dead in the ground

when iron bends in the ironsmith's hand
harvesters hold sabers in close embrace

followers in a funeral procession waver east and west
so far away, translation's sounds in May's grain waves

trees are watching the distance that will marry them off
the cattle are holding in their shit in resistance to the movements
    of the sky

(1989)

In England
在英格兰

after the church's spire and the city's chimneys sink below the
    horizon
England's sky is darker than a lover's whisper
two blind accordionists walk by, heads bowed

without farmers, no evening prayers
without gravestones, no people reciting
two newly planted rows of apple trees pierce my heart

it's my wings that have made me famous, it's England
that makes me arrive in the place that had lost me
memory, but leaves no more furrows

shame, that's my address
in all of England, there isn't one woman who can't kiss
in all of England, there's no room for my pride

from mud hiding under a fingernail, I
recognize my country — mother
has been packed in a parcel, and sent far away

(1989–1990)

Sea Watching

看海

having watched the winter sea, what flows in the veins can be
　　blood no more
so you must look out at the sea when making love
you must still be waiting
waiting for the sea breeze to face you once more
the breeze that must come from the bed

and that memory is, or must be
the mirage of the sea stored in the eyes of dead fish
the fishers must be off-duty engineers and dentists
the cotton in the June ground must be surgical gauze
you must be in the fields still searching for worries
the trees you pass by must have bumps on their heads
great resentments must have given you an unconventional future
because you say *must* too much
the way Indian women must bare their midriffs

the distance must not be far from where you live
the distance must not be far from Chinatown
there must be a moon that shines like spit
there must be someone saying that that is your health
the no longer important or the even more important *must*
must be kept in your heart
like that arrogant artillery shell on England's old face

watching the sea must have spent your best years
the constellations your eyes are keeping must have become coal
　　cinders

the shadow of the sea must have leaked from the seabed to
    another world
on a night when someone's got to die someone must be dying
even though the ring must not want to be long dead in the flesh
and the horse ass shot up with hormones must be raring to go
so cleaning up must be making a mess
when the bike chain's fallen off the pedaling must be furious
spring wind must be like someone with kidney stones buckling a
    green belt
the taxi driver's face must look like boiled fruit
when you go home that old chair must be young, it must

(1989–1990)

Sea Crossing

过海

we cross the sea, and where is that damned river
flowing to?

we turn, and behind us
is no life beyond

no life at all
worth being reborn time and again?

people on the boat all standing like wood
relatives breathing far underwater

clock chimes, still ringing
the longer they last, the less confident they are

on the other bank the trees are like people mid-coitus
replacing sea stars, seashells, and sea anemones

on the beach are scattered syringes, gauze,
and pubic hair — are we seeing the other shore?

so we turn around, as fruit do,
and behind us — a gravestone

sticking out of a high school athletic field
with only, only women crying for their children by the seaside

to know how long this winter has been:
without the dead, the river would have no end

(1990)

Winter

冬日

church spire warming in dusk's last glow
the fire in the church is already cold
oh, time, time

I look for what I've lost
and release what's been grasped
my used-up epitaph

I saunter through the human world
the great cosmos, parents of eternity
with prayers rising from hearts

silence and what's beyond sound
fuse into communication with winter:
the wind is a lone rider

and clouds are piles of laughing country brides
December's miraculous heartbeat
only an obsolete recitation

(1990)

Map

地图

midnight, someone is outside the window tempting you
cigarette butt wriggling like a silkworm
and on the table, a turbulent glass of water
you open the drawer, a forty-year snowstorm inside

a voice, but whose voice, is asking: is the sky a map?
you recognize the shouter's crow-black lips
you recognize him
and it's you, the old you
you recognize your head
being coughed out of the hospital window—

on the far horizon, the blacksmith and his nails shift together
the people putting out fires squeeze onto a postage stamp
madly dumping out the ocean
swimmers splash each other in the water
their swimming trunks sacks of flour
on which is printed: nails far from their homeland

a spicy scent
you sniff the storm's first message
like a cloud, you drift past meat hooks and out the butcher's back
    window
behind you, a leg remains laid out on the chopping block
you notice it's your own leg
because you've taken that step

(1990)

Them

他们

fingers stuck into pockets fiddling with change and their genitalia
they play at another way of growing up

in the stripper's jutting ass
is a tiny church, walking on three white horse legs

they see it with their noses
and their fingernails will sprout in the May ground

the yellow earth of May is piles of smooth gunpowder
which death mimics, death's reasoning being that

in the last provocation of soil by ironware in heat
they will become part of the sacrificed fields

before the dead have died the long-dead silence
kept all they understood from changing

stubbornly, they thought, they did
they gave up their youth

it kept death complete
they have applied our experiences.

(1991)

No

没有

no one to bid me goodbye
no one to bid goodbye to each other
no one to bid the dead goodbye, when the morning began

no boundary of its self

other than language, facing the land's lost border
other than the tulip's blossoming fresh meat, facing the night's
    unclosing window
other than my window, facing a language I no longer understand

no language

only light, tormenting and tormenting
that saw carving and carving into dawn
only the tulip restless, restless until it isn't

no tulip

only light, stagnant at dawn
starlight sowed in the sleeping luggage car of a speeding train
last light dripping from a baby's face

no light

I chop meat with an axe, and hear the screams of the shepherd at
    dawn
I open the window, and hear light and ice shouting at each other

screams that burst the chains of fog

no screams

only land
only land and shippers of millet know
that bird that only calls at midnight is the bird who's seen the
    dawn

no dawn

(1991)

I Read

我读着

in November's wheat field I read my father
I read his hair
the color of his tie, the thread of his pants
and his hooves, tripping over shoelaces
ice-skating while playing the violin
scrotum clenching, neck stretching to the sky from too much
    understanding
I read that my father is a horse with huge eyes

I read that my father once briefly left his herd
his jacket hanging on a bush
with his socks, and in the flickering herd
those pale rumps, like the soap women wash their bodies with
in oyster shells stripped of their flesh
I read the odor of my father's hair oil
his stench of tobacco
and his tuberculosis, illuminating a horse's left lung
I read a boy's doubts
rising from a golden cornfield
I read the age when I figure things out
the roof of the red room where grains are sun-dried is starting to
    rain
under the plow of wheat-planting season are dragged four dead
    horse legs
the horse's pelt like an open umbrella, its teeth splayed out in all
    directions
I read the faces taken away by time

I read my father's history silently rotting underground
the locusts on my father's body existing on their own

like a white-haired barber hugging an aging persimmon tree
I read my father putting me back into a horse's stomach
when I am about to turn into a stone bench in the London fog
when my gaze passes by the men walking down Bank Street

(1991)

I've Always Been Glad
for a Ray of Light in the Night
我始终欣喜有一道光在黑夜里

I've always been glad for a ray of light in the night
between the sounds of wind and of bells I wait for that light
on mornings when I haven't woken until noon
last leaves hanging on as if dreaming
many leaves entering winter
fallen leaves surrounding the trees
which collected four seasons' worth of wind from the outskirts of
    a tilted city —

who made sure the wind would forever be misunderstood as the
    center of loss
who made me listen to trees blocking the sound of wind once
    again
to force the wind to become five forced-open fingers in harvest
    time again
the wind's shadow grew new leaves from the hands of the dead
fingernails were pulled out, by hand, by a tool clenched
in the hand, a kind of shadow that was the spitting image
of a person and then spat on by the person, passed over by the
    person
that's what dispelled the last ray of light from the faces of the
    dead
and polished the light chopping into the forest even brighter

in the light of spring I walked into the light before daybreak
I saw the only tree that hates me and remembers me
under the tree, under that apple tree

in my memory the tables turned green
in the splendor of May when wings startled bones awake,
    opening toward me
I turned around, grass growing all over my back
I woke, and the sky was moving
the death written on my face entered into words
constellations accustomed to death shone on
death, which entered the light
to make the lonely church into the last pillar for measuring
    starlight
turning whatever slipped through into whatever was left behind.

(1991)

What Time Did I Know the Ringing Was Green
什么时候我知道铃声是绿色的

from any side of the tree I'll accept the sky
trees hide olive-green words
the way light hides in a dictionary

forsaken stars record
blinded birds balancing, light
and its shadow, death and near-death

two pears hanging, on trees
fruit bears a primal shadow
the way trees hide a ringing

on trees, December wind weathers stronger drink
a gust, urging the arrival of speech
blocked by a granary pillar, blocking

a dream dreamt by marble's bad dream, dreaming
a shock of wind sound off the tombstone, jolting
the last leaf's run to the sky

autumn writing, sprouting from tree death
ringing, shining at that moment on my face
in a sky delivering gold for the last time —

(1992)

Only Permitted
只允许

only permitted one memory
extending where the railway is powerless to reach—to teach you
to use grain to gauge the future, bolts of cloth to pave a road
only permitted one season
wheat-planting season—May sunlight
from over a naked crest, pulling land in four directions
only permitted one hand
to teach you to see with your head down—furrows in your palm
what the land has in mind flattened slowly by the other hand
only permitted one horse
paralyzed by the five p.m. women's gaze
to teach your temper, to endure your flesh
only permitted one person
the one who teaches you death is already dead
the wind will teach you to know this death
only permitted one type of death
each word is a bird with a shattered head
the sea gushes out of a clay pot smashed on the ground

(1992)

A Moment of Silence

静默

at the window awaiting the blizzard hangs your portrait
bread is served on a black plate
hands reach toward that place where no hands exist

    it is a moment of silence

at this moment snow is falling
you're being stared at by a horse
the hill covered in snow is ideas

    it is a moment of silence

quietly, a flock of sheep are moved about through the cemetery
sky thick with crows, it's daybreak
a moment of silence granted permission
records on a headstone:

    thought is what broke the moment of silence

the world outside the window does not speak
there's no speaking in an all-white landscape
the clock is ticking, the hands do not move
such is the predicament beneath a hand, on paper:

    searching for what is beyond the human

(1992)

The Boy Who Clutched a Hornet

捉马蜂的男孩

when there is no wind, there are birds
"there are birds, but there's no morning"

the boy who clutched a hornet entered from the right of the
    picture
cries of trees, taken over by birds

"little mama, your wheat field favors me"
three suns pursued one bird

"little mama, the little cow in your tummy is moving"
the blackest horse in the world galloped over

"little mama, the coffin was shipped from the south"
the trees took measure, measuring the boy's head

the child's screams were left inside a pear
even more people were left outside the frame

the child used five feet to stand
now his feet are sand

the sapling that couldn't grow leaves began to cry
an overripe plum was shouting, "you – us"

(1992)

Northern Memory

北方的记忆

absorbing winter's cold, listening to the clouds' far movements
northern trees stand in a February wind
parting, too, is standing there
reflection distant and clear in the windowpane

a midnight sweat, a downpour at dawn
in an inn in a foreign country
the wheat fields of the north begin to breathe
like cattle in a pen disturbing the earth with their hind hooves

the one alone preserves listening
but no, there is no inspiration
that could keep extorting this city
this heap of northern stones

spreading the sower's shoes toward the canvas alone
the plow has severed its ties to the ground
the way it might disdain the city for its clouds
while I use your wall to confront your vastness—

(1992)

The Things
它们

—in memoriam, Sylvia Plath

nudity is the shadow of things
like bird breath

things that are beyond this world
on the sea floor, like oysters

revealing, then shutting themselves
leaving loneliness

a loneliness that could give birth to pearls
left in the shadow of things

where memory is an iceberg
a memorial made of shark heads

a navigation to turn the sea gray
like London, a black umbrella opened

and stored inside your death
snowflakes, braille, numbers

but never memory
to make loneliness into a summoning

to make the most lonely move chairs and tables all night
make them use vacuum cleaners

to suck up the scent that keeps you
in the human world, for full on thirty years

(1993)

Locked Direction
锁住的方向

it was the laid-off locksmiths who spotted you first
when your flying rump passed through the apple tree shadow
the dim face of a cook turning toward the field

when tongues kneel, eventually kneeling in the same direction
they can't find the mouth that can speak you
they want to speak, but cannot

      to say: there are still two olives

that when kissing you can take on substance
and there is still a tongue, which can be used for a corkscrew
and there are two clouds of tomorrow, embracing on the
    riverbank
there are your kisses with somebody, becoming wild strawberries
    all over

      what does it matter that the tongues agree

it's the riddle in the corn! history decays
and marble bites your neck
the two olives, a riddle within a riddle
the magnets controlling from inside bird heads stir the ancient
    landscape
making human emptiness hover between two concrete pillars

      only the dead have souls

on a street full of black umbrellas
there is a bag heavy with tangerines about to be lifted
another sky is going to open from within an oyster murdered by
    poison
inside a horse head, a marble bathtub cracks:

green time is coming

a chicken frozen in the fridge is eager
the two raisins reliant on roast lamb legs are eager
from within unpredictable weather
from within the dripping that entices a boy to pee
from within skimmed milk
from within the last operation
eagerness and golden sand rush back into the storm together

a storm rising from the sweat glands of bacon
and armpits of violence

when floating ice keeps drifting with the posture of pregnant
    women
eager is the only word they leave behind
when your flying rump opens the unlockable direction
blocking the long night's passing with naked flesh
what word they leave behind is the sperm that passes through
    concrete —

(1994)

Unlockable Direction
锁不住的方向

it was the laid-off locksmiths who spotted you last
when your flying rump passed through the chestnut roaster's
    stupor
a cook covered his face and kneeled toward the field

when tongues kneel, eventually kneeling in different directions
they find the mouth that can speak you
but can say no more. to say, they annulled them

                    it's said: there are still two olives

that when kissing you could take on substance
it's said there is still a tongue, which can replace the corkscrew
who said there are two clouds of tomorrow, which embraced on
    the riverbank
whose kisses with somebody ever became wild strawberries all
    over

                    it doesn't matter that corn agrees

it's corn in the shadow. history decays
and a shadow of marble is biting your neck
shadows of two olives, shadows in shadow
the magnets that crack open bird heads control the sand in the
    crop
making human emptiness halt between two concrete pillars

the dead will no longer have souls

on a street that was once full of black umbrellas
there was a bag heavy with tangerines that was lifted
a sky, turned over from a big theater in an oyster murdered by
    poison
thoughts in a horse head, clear as a lightbulb filament:

green time is coming in the performance

a chicken frozen in the fridge awakes
the two raisins reliant on roast lamb legs awake
from within predicted weather
from within the dripping that keeps a boy from peeing
from within skimmed sperm
within an operation that couldn't be completed
awakening and golden sand rush back into the storm together

a storm spewing from the bathtub faucet

when pregnant women keep drifting with the posture of floating
    ice
drifting is the last word they leave behind
when your flying rump locks that unlockable direction
confessing the long night's passing with naked declamation
what sperm they leave behind is the word laid in by concrete.

(1994)

Return

归来

know the sea from the deck
and instantly know its great vacillation

know the plow from the sea, and instantly
know the bravery we had

in each instant, only from
every individual fear

forehead pushed from a forehead, standing on a threshold
to say goodbye, an instant is five years

hands in hands grasped ever tighter, say let go
and instantly the sand in the shoe all comes from the sea

just now, learning to read in the light
instantly the weight of the rucksack lightens

just now, an experience swallowing coarse bread
instantly the water in the bottle is back in the sea

stared down by the ox from my hometown, clouds
ask me to tear up, instantly I tear up

but walk in any direction
and instantly it turns into drifting

scrubbing the backs of oxen numbed by clarinets
memory instantly finds its wellspring

words instantly walk back into the dictionary
but inside words, navigation

makes the person who never navigated
live forever — yet unable to return

(1994)

Never Dream
从不做梦

make pancakes apart from the human world, use
toothmarks the child left in toast
for a bed, make another pacifier
into a bird concerned only with flight
don't cry, don't buy insurance
it's not from prayer
don't be part of this order

    never dream

be an extinguished candle in a windless night
be starlight, shining on the neck of a horseback rider
be grass that grows for only one season, make poems
be pears frozen on trees
be rye, bearing thought in the wind

    never dream

be wind, shouting at the land
be a drop of water, silently dripping
be the spasm that shoots up a horse's back
be the egg that might hatch the father
from wrested time
from insomniac time, memorial constellations
pilfer moments from riddles off the tops of heads!

(1994)

Five Years

五年

five cups of hard liquor, five candles, five years
forty-three years old, a bout of midnight sweats
fifty palms fanning at the tabletop
a flock of birds with clenched fists flying over yesterday

five strings of firecrackers crackling for May, thundering between
    five fingers
but in April four poison mushrooms parasitic on four dead
    horses' tongues didn't die
five days five hours five minutes five candles gone out
but the scenery screaming at the moment of dawn has not died
hair is dead but the tongue has not died
the temper brought back from boiled meat has not died
for fifty years mercury has seeped into semen but the semen has
    not died
the fetus who delivered himself has not died
five years have passed, five years have not died
in five years, twenty generations of insects have died

(1994)

There's No

没有

such thing as innocence, but don't criticize
that which does not glow of these things

five feet underwater, they look like hearts
still pumping blood perhaps, though with no further testimonies
like that hotel, once at the eye of the storm
wood pegs rotting in water, full once of arrowheads

    without any intent to commemorate anyone

at the breeding ground when twitch passes to sea surface
they float up, taking over the appearance of some geometric
    object
their spines requiring the least of testimonials
their pasts have no protectors. see on their faces
the depth of their wrinkles, to know of the sea
that it has never been navigated, maybe

    they are just speed

and here at this point, when dragged ashore, they
are no longer the same things — just a few philosophers' heads
not struggling anymore, no need to bundle, mingling the useless
with the necessary, sufficiently described
by their own fissures, though they disrespect the sufficient

    they are an anguish only allowed to advance

pushing the master's thoughts, intercepting silt at a further
    location
when the sea fog is blocked by invisible pillars, they
hide their possible appearances
in discoverable locations, to keep the catcher from spying

(1996)

The Light of Little Wheat

小麦的光芒

plucking cherries beloved thirty years ago, picking pears
shipped from home, chasing the arrow shooting after youth
there is another kind of longing on earth
no horse brought me here, three knocks
left on the door, people name me:
    little wheat, little wheat

        light of little wheat

walking past Chinatown's pickle seller, Korean ginseng shops,
coffin-makers, see how the first half of my life has
come out of a wheat field, the moment of shame
that is the moment of fortune, each minute and second of dusk
shining through the red silk store, as always

        light of little wheat

standing for the shovel stuck in your back, rumble
of mountains resounding in your ears, sounds
of old people's kisses, a whole plateau
smuggled into time, and still the low drumming
of northern voices, past honor, somehow all
reliant on ten thousand spinal vertebrae struck by copper
    hammers

        light of little wheat

in what quivers the only distance is the quivering of flesh
a cloud of left-hand writing, father's soul passing over
a king's dilapidated grave, squeezing into the sky whirlpool over

the wheat field
so that no matter how you pull, you can't pull apart the tangle of
    electric wires

        light of little wheat

at the intersection where the long-standing forest bowed to the
    sunset
shadows of the five grains pass over the wall, handiwork
in hand, picked up and put down again, is it
time to wipe the tears of the young? but
bear it again, bear it though it's unbearable, think
what you don't dare think, see what doesn't need seeing, trade it
with the most precious birch bark, even though it won't be traded

        light of little wheat

and that is you — the mosquito bite on your lower back
still attracts me, each drop of sweat from my body
is still a young man, you stand on my feet
and the earth still moves, when the horse blinks
the entire prairie can once again flip each one

        light of little wheat

there's always some wheat field getting all worked up, like some
female secretion, with the scent of autumn worms
turning over something made cold by its distance from
the vein of the earth — like the mole on your face
the year that died, that had to die, that must die, still
grabbed at, clawed at, clenched by bleeding fingernails
    oh the moment of clenching

        light of little wheat

when a farmer drove a horse toward regulation, the wheat field
displayed blankness, like the departure of talent
suddenly all northern foul language stopped
rice straw in horse manure flew to the sky
before the horse died, its mane having already ascended
but the horse hoofs still have their tone of voice, their grammar
    and
their premonitions: and their lines of poetry

    light of little wheat

leaning toward the wheat field where smokestacks tower
and saluting the shelterbelt of frost heaves, constellations
rise again, consoling caressing wool
horse milk rippling in the pail, criticizing
yet another morning, unfolding like this:
if it's a line of poetry, it must dynamite the dam again

    light of little wheat

lightning is a white weaver, with no concern
for the ever louder sounds of firewood chopping in the afternoon
but the jungle is a singer, singing the grass in the roof-tile gutters
known prior to me, singing the harp it was sung before
while held in the mower's arms, singing what light knew
prior to light's knowing, prior to all knowledge
    knowing all

    light of little wheat

(1996)

In a Dordogne Castle

在多多涅城堡

a watchman is eating a plum held in a handkerchief
the decrepit garden laughs
in the chamber of poetry's furnace, at midsummer
the furnace knows only burning
the happy furnace worker knows only shoveling
a woman, after walking past the shadow of a tree
has aged

her former beauty still shocks what's left of my life

(1996)

Without

没有

without expression, therefore control, from
no direction ever to have a reason again, the order of
without, which is sucked away, logic
without limit, the without
increasing, with a boat, but empty
but still crossing, so it must be with someone floating to the
    riverbed
upholding stones, offering a great river
that rises when upon meeting height, then flows into
that river that can't keep still, which will be with a metal
surface, the transparency of ice, never again mixing blood
aging, not decaying, the cornerstone will
the doubter's head will not, reason
will, pain will not, at its boiling point, love will
upholding will, waiting will not, upholding
is waiting for without
taking away and its equivalent element
before, let the people upholding
avoid being only population, horsepower means
mileage still, sand will reach
the place where it is itself, it is without around
without boundary, without rust, without

(1998)

Bearing It
忍受着

on the riverbanks of simultaneously freezing rivers
stand tall and bear it, bear it in the piss of your descendants
things are not just things, in what was
the position of people bear that others
are also people, in that season that's always depleted
always excessive, bear it
penned livestock posts are always
philosophers' heads, always mourning
time leaked out of each pronunciation's
alternating rectifications, to replace
the locations where always stand
fathers with forever flustered faces

on roads child prostitutes walked with their big feet
bear the road, in wall-hitting sound of thought
after sustained training sucks it away, bear it
this is how time is given, forecast
from a cyst in a horse leg, bending
the iron nails in manure, not
turning back into yeast, a pair
of bells being rung more urgently underground
than in the ovary, bearing together
the dirge, when it always faces forward

where sand still misses the melon patch
bear the thunder, weaker than the whispers
of cotton pickers, what can be spoken no more
makes what can be heard no more into what cannot be calmed

the trace of the moment of wind, the wheat field under ten
    thousand needles
the north that can make coins crack, still teaching
them to be the same age as the annual cold current
they who stick their feet out even in stone
mask their faces even in statues, and when
someone rolls their hands into trumpets, bear it—

                                        (1998)

Wait

等

bird catcher's memories played by a sawed-off piccolo
your calls from the spot furthest from foreheads
close into a sky that cannot feel pain

which must be the sky of love

wait for the table split by the drunkard's fists to rejoin, birds
smelling the armchair with folded hands
from which still seeps the scent of wood's depths

which must be your scent

wait for the hands in the picturesque landscape to stop massaging
the sunflowers pecked clean by birds still face
the direction of their nature, which must be

the maturity they are powerless to endure

wait for flying birds' eyes, faces shut, to reproduce stars
the way they were a hundred million years ago, have the river
that flowed through and reflected your face

leave a little value, mother —

(1998)

As

既

despair as nightingale, you must sing in ivory's echo
but may not ask how long until you can become a butterfly

so while scratching in the boatman's armpit, go conduct the
    orchestra
go pick the lemons floating in the score, help ice
open fish ponds, drink after horses from discarded bathtubs
raise your head in processed spaciousness, and
shine the blue as deep as the hospital a little brighter, while
    running on
the tips of burning matches
follow each instant, and become tradition right away

(1998)

Whose Forgotten Weather Is This
这是被谁遗忘的天气

meaning nothing about it will ever be recalled
nor will anything be worth recurrent vanishing

the painted eyes on the boat look ahead
on the road, only horses return

just then, rolling clouds
suddenly catch up with the pipe organ roar

every instant of defeat surges into it
keys no longer need to speculate, thunder is never empty

the ocean doesn't only count sand, some people
still write letters, but no longer send them —

(1998)

Courtyard Home

四合院

raindrops detained in the eaves
remind, in the occasion of autumn, that old friends and old
    stories
have knocked open the acorns of generations of front doors

all over the courtyard

each gust of wind plunders comb teeth once
a cabinet painted out of ox blood
could be a hairband's rat teeth, an old scent

that cannot be gotten rid of

the old room hides scales and not clocks, but how many
myths does it hide, only roof tiles picked up back onto
the body, surnames heavier than given names

musical instruments

have long stopped performing in the world of dust, five saws
put back in the drawer, ten golden bowls rung against foreheads
no borrowing of the bell toll, so no transmission

apricot blossoms on their heads

braiding each other's hair, four girls
sit around a willow, the gods seen
years ago removed with the fishtank

indicating stone horses

cherry blossoms on the branch, no need
to count one by one, only shadows
of being at the same moment as mother

the moon fills the bed

at the age when to dream is to read the paper
when autumn pears hit each other over old sheet music, cut off
by someone once, strung up as words

stone coffin wood cart ancient road urban infrastructure

over the ridges of low-rise roofs, the logic of
the courtyard home, street grids, whose
palmprint prophesied it into a square

a cold of misbuttoned coats

change in the hand, scattered on the table
laid out to the old city's crumbling stone steps
then gathered as

more joy is dropped

gently carry the father of latter years onto your knee
face him in the direction of the ancients washing their morning
    faces
the calling of the knife-sharpeners in the *hutong* comes along

looking raises the walls once more

(1999)

In Tunis

在突尼斯

the desert is out of shape, so the wind must have
met a right angle, and there are promises to keep
so what's learned must be less than what's lost
what slips through the hourglass less still
while what's sticking out
will enter whatever weather comes later
in a place that looks more a city
the more evenly distributed its sandstorms

that unthought and unspoken, unmade
but unshroudable fate, like how
every side of the old city leads to a shoe store
where here is there, where where
is everywhere, and in the Phoenicians' place of origin
the sight of men carrying whole cowhide
is covered by palms asking for money

that is the signal of existence emitted
when the pouring of wastewater under
the crack in the door sharpens the stench: if
someone comes here just to take away sunlight
what gets taken away must be a longing
especially the moment the broker puts in a glass eye
against tin-gray skies, there's always somebody
to aim more nervously than horse bookies:
the hate shot from a masked woman's eyes
amasses her whole body's beauty, as if
bending thought, yet also bending to thought

(2000)

Thanks

感谢

when returning it borrow it
thanks to the vacant land, for it is in fact the land

the coal region expands its geography toward workday's end
thanks to its past, for it looks particularly spacious

on the line where ancestral skeletons refuse to become stone
statues
thanks to the trees for standing still, for it is the standing-still of
relatives

no more tombstones gauging undulating underground water
levels
thanks to them for being such good reciters

bowing toward where bestowal continues to take place
thanks to the deeper meaning of the earth for passing to the knees

to push forward where blessing doesn't know where to go
thanks to hidden mileage for beginning

when empty land displays the wheat field
thanks to the predetermined apology, for it has not been taken
away

trees' lyrical power repeatedly leads our lapels
thanks to the resplendent starlight at the bridge, for pointing to
where the recipient is hiding —

(2000)

Writing That Can't Let Go of
Its Grief Examines the Cotton Field
不放哀愁的文字检查棉田

bronze has exiled the witness's tongue
grass relates the incompetence of words

after hearing the family leave with their antibodies
the ripping left by the twig fence is unheard

river and riverbed in endless litigation
the bitter woman has kneeled on the embankment white and
    clean

see the bowl-holding statue standing forever
driving out locusts with collective pacing

the river engages once again in the explanation of blood
the weak who despise the journey will have only mileage

(2000)

From Behind the Horse Radiating the Eyelashes of Lightning
从马放射着闪电的睫毛后面

sun rising in the east, shining on the horse's incisors
the horse's eye rims hold my tears

in the horse's flaring nostrils, there's me
at fifteen firing a gun at a fire-red crop field

leaning on broken neck wheat straw, the horse
shrinks, its head risen just to the level of rising sorrow

one half-buried horse
makes the wilderness look even broader

my head hangs between death and prostration
hear the clippety-clop of horse tears in the depths of the forest

butterflies are overflowing the horse brain
a golden wheat field stares at me

at the first meeting, the horse's forehead
and mine butted each other

the sound of horse hooves spreads from the earth's core
as the horse keeps searching for the world of dust for me

(2000)

Ahead
前头

parting forever there, it's already gone
wherever they built it, there it is

(because there is no terminus)

wherever a neglected vacant lot might be
it will not be ahead

(no, it must be one's own order)

no place left to be lost in
(no hell, no wilderness, no sangha)

what's past is all there is
what's passing already is not
what's partial therefore is not
the borderless can nevermore be broad

(logic has no limit)

wheat is no longer wheat

(when no more is one of its seasons)
our doctors will nevermore be peasants
(so there aren't any excuses)
what can be embraced is obsolete
(outside words, there are no ideals)
the value is in making anyone hurt

(but for any college
the no – it must also be a new grave)

so sing: there will be no more choruses
(no choruses)

no rhythm will piece it together
with neither the strength to prop up the zither, nor any more
    submission
(so there aren't any obstacles)
it still has its fate, no more bridges
when the stone figure waves, parting doesn't move
(so even comparison has halted)
anthropoids will periodically utter human sounds:

the no – it travels farther than the hymns

(2001)

Promise

诺言

I love, love that my shadow
is a parrot, that I love to eat
what it loves to eat, that I love to give you what I don't have
I love asking, do you still love me
I love your auriculae, that they love to hear: I love adventure

I love aroused rooms inviting us to lie down as their roof
I love lying on my side, casting a shadow for a straight line
casting a string of villages for a voluptuous body
I want the mole nearest your lip
to know, this is my promise

I love that the intelligence in my dreams is an ambitious groom
I love eating raw meat, staring straight at hell
but I still love secretly playing the violin in your embrace
I love putting out the lights early, and waiting
for your body to relight the room

I love that when I go to sleep, the pillow is covered in plums
and that when I wake, the plums go back to their branches
I love that the waves attract the forward deck all night long
I love to shout: you'll be back
I love tormenting the port like this, and tormenting words

I love controlling myself before the table
I love sticking my hand in the sea
I love spreading my five fingers out at once
to grab tightly to the edge of the wheat field

I love that my five fingers are still your five boyfriends

I love that memory is a life a bit less
but still more than what a woman misses when
walking toward me, as if that girl with the violin case
thirty years ago, on the street, in the dusk
were still smiling at me for no reason

and I love even more that we are still a pair of torpedoes
waiting for someone to shoot us again
I love joining with you in the depths of the sea, that you
are mine, only mine, I still
love to say it, love to sing my promise —

(2001)

I Dream

我梦着

dreaming of my father, a cloud that writes left-handed
with the thickness of pharmacy glass
he is wearing a blue raincoat
on the street where the old record needle turned
past the laundry, the coffin dealer
not far from the street I walked toward growing up on
his blue skeleton still trying to hail a cable car

at every intersection I dream of, there's a father
in the background of a wrangling pile of fathers
every street resisting, every corner
bearing witness: at the crossroads
a father's tongue is yanked out
like a bicycle tire inner tube . . .

the whole time since my father died rushes by at full speed
I wish someone could end this dream
wish someone would wake me
but there's no one, and I keep dreaming
as if I were in some dead man's dream
dreaming of his life

spade after spade of earth is shoveled into the men's bare chests
from their bodies, dreams give the earth new boundaries
a swarm of flies that will bite no longer
rose out of there some time ago
but seeing that big scale swinging idly in the fish shop
they will wail and cry in unison . . .

I accept this dream
I have dreamt what I should dream of
I have dreamt of dream's command

as if I'd been kidnapped by the dream—

(2001)

In the Fog That's Left Only to Us

在一场只留给我们的雾里

1

we have no way anymore to imagine how you were when young
perhaps because of distance, which made you just one genre

the point is like your death
staying at high latitude, your memory in Bretagne
your past becoming an architecture
any point of which we lean against, to say:
your wheels are only used for swinging

like asking, rarely passing through your words
but always with reason, as long as it can be put to speech
it will enter your tones, sealing all directions
save raiding rhythm, giving nothing
only passing, directly entering English
may tireless things replace your imitators
for truth, or else for the pursuit of truth

once written down, it can still slip away
and that is all that you prefer not to see
your aversion is discovered
thus leaving what's secondary in the metaphor:
your encounters wear us down, too

2

literature has gone far amid grand exegesis
as if attending a funeral where no one has died
or puncturing lifeless syntax

at any event, speed means not much is doable
though to stop would be to shame it
the last in a line of stone figures
is always new, and we must look askance
to see the prophet at the end
if it was ever you for a time
then not now, as before words
get denigrated, they've already turned into something else
and meaning always stays precise
at least, above two tones
we are the same as you in that we're strangers
this is our only precondition
when all orphans' faces are so similar
in the fog that's only left to us, stop looking

(2001)

Peeping Through a Keyhole at a Koninginnedag Horse
从锁孔窥看一匹女王节的马

stretching the in-between distance of trees, or shrinking
horse tail trailing, the horse head coerces the course

the former makes language fodder, the latter
will be bound with the freedom to wait for what's paid

sprinting, simultaneously to the front and the back
with the shadows of trees, the shadow of the horse

fills in the shadow of bronze, that's how power's shadow is
when seen from the standpoint of rusted fog

only sprinting no longer counts as sport
judged from the higher side of the tree:

it's sprinting that makes the horse, and that mounts the horse
so neighing speaks loudly, so shade conquers rule

if the two join to disappear
well, then disappearance cannot be taught

swear on the land being plowed into comprehensibility:
this is what the eyes of an eleven-year-old boy have divulged to
    me

(2001)

Don't Ask

别问

don't ask between which leaves to come near me
writing letters for some afternoon some day some month some
    year

don't ask from which side to enter the writing on the sail
the letter is still a piece of paper, for now

don't ask who's closest to October, you or me
the year has come beating its wings from the forest of overripe
    persimmons

don't ask which branch tip December found its riddle on
the ray of light brightening the last leaf set out so long ago

don't ask if twice surpasses once
the question will turn the moment into noon and dawn and also
    dusk

don't ask when the archaeopteryx fossil will speak
believe what the phoenix believes

the first sound passes into the long gone —

(2002)

Not Mourning Language   The Report of a Cannon Is the Start of Comprehension

不对语言悲悼　炮声是理解的开始

so command thunder like this — no sound
no explaining the wolf, no — another round of salvos

    let history lie, let the deaf monopolize listening
    words load nothing

thunder isn't thunder, silence is thunder
no understanding — out of it crawls the most unyielding culture

    no understanding, so the sea is vast beyond measure
    no understanding, so the four seas are one

                                     (2003)

Fast, Faster, Call
快, 更快, 叫

the clock stops at the second of the vow
calling the edge to continually rise, to ascend

calling back every day that's passed, to
change locks – year, last year, every year

each vocal part is calling
calling the bird that must be the phoenix

the too late calling the too early
calling in our language

the bulk future – another season in the sound of the call
calling from over another piece of equipment

calling for those who sing of our homelands to cry
cry from the dead, but from you – to sing!

(2003)

In a Few Modified Sea-Jumping Sounds

在几经修改过后的跳海声中

—in memoriam, Sylvia Plath

take a child who's been rinsed in water, dawn
interrupted between thunder and words
a shadow cutting newspaper into seven sections
two rows of teeth, flickering light from a street lamp
shooting moonlight, shooting the all new dust

in the wave's newest accent, pushing
a frozen herdsman and deep-sleeping rhythm
blood barges beyond ramparts, with broken noises from primitive
    chapters:
between prayer and wreckage
words choose wreckage

on the sea swells a wall of wave over wave
on the street, sincere people standing still
emulate tulips with severed necks
pain has more clarity than language
the sound of farewell travels farther than that of goodbye

each irrefutable entrance in the mountains is unlatched
the gardening daughter's expanding silhouette shuts
the sea is composed of endless cobblestones
a humanity without a world converges there
no sail, no shadow, and no billows

until the internal sound of words comes
pain, pain that never passes
will find life's ferocious exit
for a long time the swan song will follow echoes
the purest death will never be back

(2003)

The Light of Vermeer
维米尔的光

in proportion to its Zen, a little scale
weighs the dust in a ray of light
against the weight of dust's oversignification

each tiny pearl, touched
by a golden-pupiled girl
carries a shine even tinier

so extract numbers, teach numbers
so as to learn song — however late, however long
to arrive at the light of Vermeer

never enounced, thus so beautiful

(2004)

DELUSION IS THE MASTER OF REALITY
(1982–1988)

Delusion Is the Master of Reality
妄想是真实的主人

and we, we are birds touching lip to lip
in the story of time
undertaking our final division
from man

the key turns in the ear
the shadows have left us
the key keeps turning
birds are reduced to people
people unacquainted with birds

(1982)

Captured Wild Hearts Always Side with the Sun
被俘的野蛮的心永远向着太阳

but the partition, the partition comes only from accompaniment
    and caresses
  partitions of familiarized knowledge
  the loved and the discriminated against
  always one woman
  becoming the enemy who shames our memory

release it, release what pain can be remembered
guard it, guard and release this promise
    the weaker the more trusted
the heart that brokers no trade with time is always in childhood

each scream eliminates a pain
and must, must cultivate acquired habits
more complicated people must remind us
    to face the more profound enemies
and especially not to remember how we were caressed
what is communicated is but inconsequential language

    tomorrow, and then tomorrow
    we have no memory of tomorrow
tomorrow, the gifts we exchange will be just as savage
sensitive hearts never trade with tomorrows
captured wild hearts always side with the sun
    always side with the wildest face —

(1982)

News of Liberation's Exile by Spring

解放被春天流放的消息

open the rose-gold throat
    but do not divulge
that forever, forever is an abstruse word

    of course is of course is the sun
    clumsy boiling flesh
is the enthusiastic instrument helping sound to rise
in the first blast of a trumpet blown by the scorching sun

    is the first miracle of lips birds peck open

in the deeper deeper trust in story
we plant every day, pick every day
having used the fields and taken their secrets
    their used lust
    was the grain we saved each day
    despicable aphoristic attentiveness
    has been seeping into our hearts since then
    the appearances we were forced to surrender
    have become enemy weapons

and birds, birds are unwilling to carry away our forms

when days of memory have no more commemorative days
hearts hungry for praise agree with ruthless hearts
roses that love yogurt turn into roses clamoring for war
    and what is always, always
    used to broadcast viciousness
    gets rewritten into the first news of spring—

(1982)

His Whole Past Is in a Story
一个故事中有他全部的过去

when he opens the windows of his body facing the sea
toward the clanging of ten thousand steel knives
his whole past is in a story
when all the tongues stick themselves out toward this sound
to pick up ten thousand clanging knives
all days squeeze into one day
so each year becomes a day longer

the final year collapses under a great oak tree
his memories come from a cattle pen, above which motionless
    smoke sits in the sky
boys who've caught fire hold hands around a kitchen knife,
    singing
before the flames are extinguished
they roll burning above the trees
the flames hurt his lungs

as his eyes are holidays from two opposing cities
nostrils grand tobacco pipes greeting the skies
women fire at his face with love
so his lips might maintain their gap
in a moment, a train running opposite death will pass
so his outstretched arms might maintain their morning
and press down the head of the sun

a soundless handgun declared the morning's arrival
a morning chillier than an empty basin upside down on the
    ground
a creaking of branches broken off in the forest
a broken-off bell clapper on a door unloading onto funereal
    streets

his whole past is in a story
death has become one unnecessary heartbeat

when the stars fall full speed to an earth in search of snake venom
time is rotting outside the clock's tick-tock
rats lose their teeth on the rust spots of a copper coffin
fungus stomps its feet on decaying lichen
for a long time the cricket's son does needlework on his body
and evil, it rips up his face on a drum
internally he's all the glory of death
all of it, his whole past is in a story

his whole past is in a story
the first time the sun read his eyes from up close
a closer sun sat on his lap
a tall thin man takes a rest, sitting down on a chopped-off tree
    stump
with the sun smoking between his fingers
every night I aim at it with my telescope
until the instant the sun goes out
and the tree stump rests where he had been sitting

more silent than bok choy patches in May
the horse he rode walked by in the morning
death has shattered into a heap of pure glass
the sun now rolling thunder on the pallbearer's path home
as the child's tender feet walk out on evergreen olive branches
but my head is swollen, as if ten million horse hooves were
    pounding drums
compared to a bulky machete, death is just a grain of sand
which is why his whole past is in a story
which is why millennia are turning their faces — look

(1983)

In a Northern Fallow Field Is
a Plow That Pains Me
北方闲置的田野有一张犁让我疼痛

in a northern fallow field is a plow that pains me
when spring falls over like a horse off an
empty hearse
a head made of stone
gathers the storms of death

scrubbed by a storm's iron hair
under a hat
there is a blank space — the time after death
has removed his face:
a red-brown beard reaches out
to gather the long fallow dignity of the north

it's spring that bites on his heart like a bell
like the plop of a child's head sinking to the bottom of a well
like a child boiling over roiling fire
his pain — like a giant's

sawing on upside-down timber
is like sawing your own leg
a sound more frail than grief's silk thread
passes through a shutdown lumberyard passes through
the lumberyard's lonesome warehouses
it is the lonesomeness of the sower reaching the end of the field

a flax-colored peasant woman
waves, though she has no face

to the plowman to the bent-over back
a rusted mother has no memory
but waves — like a stone
that comes from a far-off ancestor

(1983)

Seeing from Death's Direction

从死亡的方向看

from death's direction you will always see
people you should never see
you'll always casually bury a place
casually sniff around, then bury yourself there
in that place they'll hate

they throw the dirt in their shovels on your face
and you should thank them — and be thankful again
that your eyes will see no more enemies
and even if they send the screams from when they fell into enmity
from death's direction
you will never hear
those screams of absolute pain

(1983)

The Smoke from Dawn's Gun Curls Upward
黎明的枪口余烟袅袅

smoke from dawn's gun curls upward
the music of the stove fire's nightlong morning light, all dreaming

with delicate claws I rub cobblestones
the night mouse is like a child

walk the silver white earth into a rustle
oh all dreaming

but the morning has shone on the past's bright mirror
everything everything has its age

and the orchard shines the home's door and windows red

everything everything has its age
but the wheel of passion doesn't stop in any season

listen, I hold the night mouse, the trumpets covering its body all
    pouting
listen, the night mouse stands on the roof of the train singing
    with pride:

in a place where there's only happiness
happiness is like timber

happiness is like timber
cricking and crackling

and the orchard shines the home's door and windows red

(1983)

The Ill

病人

three years ago the tones stopped
the empty ring scratched the glass surface
a chip of the sky
cut down speech
from the window

it would never make a noise again
outside the window words disperse
look at them and they turn into apples
their flesh having soaked in all sound
smoke always wants to go back to wherever it was emitted from

in the three years since I planted a tree
in the pit
often someone with a beautiful face
has come to stand before it
seeing someone who wants to scoff at me approaching
the fallen leaves cover up the pit

(1984)

The Construction of Language
Comes from the Kitchen
语言的制作来自厨房

if the construction of language comes from the kitchen
then the heart is the bedroom. they say
if the heart is the bedroom
then delusion is its master

from the delusion expressed by birds' eyes
the boy manipulating the plunger mute
admits: *agitato*
is like a temperament

a brain that cannot dream
is just the badlands of time
the boy manipulating the plunger mute admits
but cannot understand:

the contracepted seed
doesn't produce form
each seed is a reason . . .
a reason that wants saying

is like an address
saying nothing, a wild man smoking cigarettes
will press walnuts saying nothing
into the tabletop. they say

all commentary
must stop — when
horses all around are so quiet
when they observe the eyes of humans

(1984)

The Song

歌声

the song, it is the song cutting down the birch grove
silence like a snowstorm pouring down
every birch tree remembers my song
I hear the song that gives the world rest
and I'm the one demanding it rest
covered in the costume of a snowstorm
I'm the one standing in the center of silence
as silent as the stopping of snow
even in this pear is a silence
it's my song that once made all the stars in the sky go dark
I'll never again be starlight in the sky above the grove

(1984)

Longevity

寿

reliving a heart's quiver in the season bees make honey
I hear the seed's breathing then open my eyes
the spots on the back of the milk cow shift with the shadows of
    the sun
ah the sun, the fruit of god
with god's hand the fruit-filled golden basket
— a horse shuts fortunate eyelids
like a school of fish seeing the beauty of the fisherman's face

just now it was just right: summer this year
a train got its legs cut off the conductor
walked in the field. a watermelon in the field
was giving off steam. the ground is covered with the sun's nails
and hens were selling eggs in the sunlight
the moon's facula came from the sky's typewriter
a horse took down its mask, made completely of bone
and the sky got widely bright. who knew what it was waiting for?

all commentary stopped — coming from
the guidance of ancient breasts and seven pitchforks
sleep and some hard edibles
in a horse's pink brain: the ocean rushes in through the window
its waves are rotten, and the inner organs of things surrender
because they have no capacity for shame
sap's thin drip is interrupted
the big tree retrieves the sun's shadow from the ground
the tiny bus station still laying out yesterday's chessboard

a seed returns to the depths of memory. the universe
in the fox-hunter's narrow eye
and a tangerine's memory bleeding on his forehead
he hears their voices
it's the sound of them turning into cement

(1984)

When Fifteen
十五岁

sowing steel when fifteen
overripe crops shot guns

the earth's head was covered with a blanket
the world grew a big bump

struggle was a big mop
always cleaning though it couldn't see blood

a belly of summer wide open
all fools' heads were held high

the world was a big ambush
the world was a big baby

opening ruthless eyes:
sometimes a beginning needs bleeding

sometimes a beginning will be used to stop the bleeding
kicking new leather shoes into the tree when fifteen

darkness held tight onto the
claw tip that stretched ahead

(1984)

Horse

马

dark gray clouds are like pallbearers
carrying a sorrowful ox head behind the pasture

lonely stars huddle together
like a blizzard

suddenly appearing on grandmother's frightening face
as the little white mouse was playing with its feet

the wild prince coughing up blood galloped across the dark
    prairie
the old world's last knight

−horse
a headless horse, running

(1985)

Knack
技

for a hundred years as soon as nightfall condenses each day
sunset's ancient determination descends the red wall
to remake gold — and the ardor of rust corroding red copper

causes time's elapse to be like words
sowing a splash of nothingness, "quietude"
leaning on a plateau
— a whiff of iron

ruins like wordless words

through the wordless
slithers a snake-shaped map
bass flowers tremble, wool pattern multicolor

clock's kingdom erect, like a hated allegory:

a silent snowstorm unstopped for a hundred years,
an unclear world supplying us with shivers
stand up on a sunset-infatuated lead-leaf roof
to read effects a miracle —
the holy is a wordless stare:

a colorful stone corridor appears, river water measuring the
    riverbed
a python tattoo
casts off the picture in the leopard's eye

psychic strength usorious of autumn fruit's ripe brilliance

(1985)

Dead. Ten Dead

死了。死了十头

Ten more. Ten
more lions

posthumous affairs: neither many
nor few — precisely

ten rigor mortis
tongues. Like five pairs

of misshapen wooden sandals
ten rusted

tails
like ten veterinary assistants

with ten ropes loosed
from their hands. Twenty

dreaming eyelids open:
in a bath sit

ten lions, mute
but alive. But what's dead

— a story starved to death

by ten lions. The story
coming from ten

storytelling
meddlesome throats.

(1985)

Northern Voice

北方的声音

so much vastness and expansiveness uniting, using their lungs
their front claws, turning backward, to lie on their chests
their breathing, accelerating winter warmth
though they love using the cold even more —

and I grew up in a windstorm
the windstorm held me and helped me breathe
like a child inside my body crying
I want to understand his cries like using a harrow plow on myself
every grain of sand opens its mouth
mother doesn't let the river cry
    but I admit this voice
    could dominate all authority!

some voices, even all of them
are used for being buried
we walk on the tops of their heads
underground they recover their robust gasps
a ground with no feet and so no footsteps
but which is rumbling forward
    all language
will be crumbled by this wordless voice!

(1985)

It's

是

it's   that great fabric
dawn trampled on at the horizon
it's the instant both
nighttime and daytime claim
it's first light   through a damaged metal wall
revealing a disfigured   face
    I love you
    I'll never take it back

it's   the stove leaning   the sun collapsing on the mountain ridge
loneliness sprinting to the fissure
it's wind
a blind mailman   walking into the depths of the earth's core
its green blood
wiping away all sound   I believe
in the words it takes away:
    I love you
    I'll never take it back

it's the songs of the past   a string of staring bells
it's the sound of the river's handcuffs
beating a small drum
it's your blue eyes two suns
descending from the sky
    I love you
    I'll never take it back

it's two hammers   taking turns striking

firelight from the same dream
it's the moon   heavy as a bullet
sinking the boat we rode in
it's mascara   that never runs
   I love you
   I'll never take it back

it's everything lost
swollen into a river
it's flame   flames are another river
flames   eternal hooks
hooks claws all pointing upward
it's the form of flame
crackling   cracking on the star-shaped
outstretched   yet continually burning fingers

I love you
I'll never take it back

(1985)

The October Sky

十月的天空

the October sky floats above the milk cow's amnesiac face
a newborn lawn bows to May earth, sobbing accusations
hands grab soil and clog horse ears, hear how
between dark strata someone's walking by way of fingernails!

likewise, my five fingers are a fictitious plum tree
my legs are a plow half-kneeling in the soil
I follow the sounds of the shovel
and work hard

to bury the weeping deep underground
to bury the auditory beside the weeping:
right under the casket
we bury the sky we saw when young

the thin air seduces me:
face after face, slowly sinking
face after face, rising from old faces
to struggle is to trade lives!

at the horizon of furrowed sunflower brows gray clouds are
    rolling
how many hands destroyed by thunder, how many heads that
    have chopped off wind
go to sleep now, field, and hear how
the weeds resound with gilded chimes

(1986)

Care
关怀

morning, the sound of a bird's stomach speaking
wakes its mother. before waking (how to fall asleep
with a field painted on a blood pillow)
the bird, that little finger sticking up out of a branch
its head is a shining gold chisel
and its mouth a ray of shovel-shaped light
flips a pupa buried in the strata
"come, let's plant
    the care of the world together!"

the bird sings in a child's voice
and with an obstinate head researches a kernel
(in which is contained eternal hunger)
on the face of this sixteen-year-old bird
two terrible black eyes
are a pair of upside-down binoculars
from which clumsy hunters are shot
—a crowd of swaying college students
and on their backpacks is written: eternal solitude.

looking at the world from between her fingers, mother
locks her hair into the cabinet
a bolt of ugly lightning contorts her face
(not unlike the prospect of growth rings meditating in trees)
a snowstorm that shakes ten million white hands
is falling, and on the snow-covered ground
two sets of tortuous tracks

a short person looks like a black coat
walking the filthy field into aggravation

and so, abruptly, from the strata of the walnut
from a wheat field
I know my own heart:
a stupid turbulence of blood
a caress as of milk
I drink down this morning
this morning is when I arrive.

(1986)

Gravestone

墓碑

black morning of Scandinavian study
ice sweeps the boundless sea
winter scenery fills the heart
that's how strong are the memories you need to endure.

listening to the dignified stroll of snow on roofs
how many generations end by plowing and weeding at dusk
hollow sunlight swaps with silence in lamps
this night, people will sympathize with death and mock sounds of
    crying:

    thought so weak
    thinkers even weaker

a neat note rolls over the snow-covered wilderness like tank tread
twelve dumb birds, knocked out on the ground
a century's fools discussing the shocks they've gotten:
a picture of a field outside the sheet of paper.

wearing an old coat walking out of the forest, using
a wrecked field to cover remorseful faces
you, a king in a village
alone demanding words from depression

demanding them from your own answers

(1986)

Words

字

they are autonomous
clambering together
to resist their own meanings
read them and they murder point-blank
every morning I get angry at these things
I hate these things that as soon as they're
written are his writing

the dreams I've had
are gas leaked from his head
a composure behind having
plucked the last good tooth
quivering on his face
like a patient who's forgotten to get a blood transfusion
he rushes out the door
he's looked down on himself for a long time

(1986)

Moving House
搬家

on an afternoon when winter rats ice-skate in every direction
I've decided whether to move house or not
I'll let the nails rest
picture frames loaded on a sled
the desk moved to the center of a field
I hadn't realized so many people were standing at the horizon
everyone's hand is the handlebar of a stretcher

what were they carrying—the land's meat
shook like gold, I hadn't realized
the trees on all sides were copying me
wearing a black shirt up top
and underneath on their bare trunks
written: forest for sale

(1986)

Windmill

风车

the eternal wheel revolves all over
I'm the one that doesn't spin
like decadent architecture paralyzed in the field
I'm yearning for the wild wind's arrival:

those more grave than pain
rumble on over, ruling my head
thunder in the sky weaves while galloping
the sky is like stones, fantasizing after they crumble
tails keeping busy on a butt
cattle and sheep squeezed into a pile, fleeing
it's these things, piled as memory
that make me hold the shriek of darkness
close to me again . . .

but our bad fortune, our master
stands at the end of a field made of flesh
and with his frightening face continues to applaud the storm —

(1986)

Do You Love the Jingling Field
你爱着叮当作响的田野吗

consigning flesh to the dark night's horse
using nudity to obstruct the long elapse of the night
and adjusting the sower's gait
sparks flew from the plow

that was when my form
gushed in

the instant the sawman cracked the dawn in two

the sharp bull horn braced against the cliff wound
your eyes allowed in all the evening
my speech melted in your mouth
two lips healing the sky

that lodged wheat field
continues our existence

(1986)

Remade

改造

remake language with remade tools
with remade language
keep remaking

every generation
grabs at what's on the table
until this generation

he
just reaches out
and the girls start laughing

when he realizes it
he starts laughing along
which makes it all funnier:

he just reaches out
the water stops flowing
he removes his hand

now the water won't flow

(1987)

My Uncle
我姨夫

when I look down from the toilet of a childhood of high-up
    shithouses
my uncle is staring down a bull
in their common gaze
I think I see an aim:
that all light located in shadow may have nowhere to hide!

when a flying soccer field passes over the school
the possibility of reality's dissolution
enlarges my uncle's eyes
they could see the sun freezing over the arctic sky
and my uncle would use tweezers — to pluck it back into history

so I believe the sky is mobile
my uncle often comes back from there
in the paces of a designer walking out of his designs
and so I believe even more: with the sound of an opening door
    my uncle
shuts himself off — with a kind of flashback

my uncle will repair the clock
as if he had inhaled enough premonition beforehand
the error he wants to correct
has been completed by missed time:
so we will be reduced wholesale to the liberated!

the scent of tobacco steeping in the clouds still chokes me
in the disappeared direction of streetcar tracks

I saw my uncle's beard growing in a wheat field
my uncle was ahead wearing a red kerchief
running out of the earth—

(1988)

The Road to Father
通往父亲的路

a chairback warped from twelve seasons of sitting, the whole way
slapping my hand swollen looking over a wheat field
winter's handwriting, growing out of ruined ash

someone in the sky cries: "buy all the
shade the clouds cast over the field ridge!"
a severe voice, mother's

mother walks out of her last will
cloaked in snow
using a climate to seize a cabin

within which is that famous countryside:
a boy with golden eyelash splinters is kneeling
digging up my wife: "don't ever die again!"

and me, I kneel behind the boy
digging up my mother: "it's not because of no more love!"
behind me kneel my ancestors

in a line with saplings about to become chairs
ascending into callous outer space
picking weeds. behind us

kneels a somber planet
wearing iron shoes looking for signs of birth
before going back to digging — on the road to father

(1988)

Northern Land

北方的土地

always counting pulses, watching the river flow
always leaning on a wood table, thinking of snow
the axe sound and the locusts that split firewood
are always touching permafrost in winter, feet
maintaining, I belong here
I belong here, I record, I gauge, I feed
the apparatus raw meat, I maintain: here, right here
    always here —

in a country with a stone king towering back to the sun
on a thrashing floor, in an empty classroom on break
before snow starts out from the deepest point of the sky
fifty bad clouds, passing over the heads of cotton pickers
one hundred old women, flying beyond the sky
one thousand boys, standing at the horizon taking a piss
one hundred million planets, continuing in their desolation
one century —

the ancestors' somber complexion, shading rows of statues
stones set within their distance
in the birch grove hang black wool coats
a reaping woman's red scarf tied on an ear of wheat
    seasons, seasons
with undying discipline
plant us in the road that history goes down —

always in this season, this extraneous season
winter's reading slows, the field's pages

unturning, each reader's head
sinking into secrecy — the thrill after attaining openness

    northern land
your desolation rests in the pit that's digging you
your memory dug away
your expanses wither
from lack of grief, while you are grief itself

    wherever you are, there is grief
from the forehead of that failed wheat field
twelve acres of corn field, still and soundless
weaker than weeds, you can no longer hear
what you need to tell yourself, keep pouring:
    "that is your gospel . . ."

(1988)

September

九月

September, a blind man walks ahead feeling wheat waves,
    buckwheat
emitting the aroma of parable
— the sky twenty years ago

slipping past a profile of a youth reading
I open the window and see trees, standing still
reciting recollections: there is an empty patch in the forest

crumbled petals scatter as they fall
finding on the master's face their eternal resting place
a gust of old wind makes me bow

September clouds, turned into compost heaps
the dark before the rainstorm, sorting out the sky
and covering it with a handkerchief for wiping tears

mother bows her head to mow the grass, tailors bury their heads
    in work
the books I read in the evening
transform into black earth once more

(1988)

The Ringing

钟声

no bell tolls to remind of memories
but today I heard
a total of nine clangs
I don't know if there were any more
I heard them when I was walking out of the stable
and I'd walked a mile
before I heard something else:
"when, in striving for circumstances
did you increase your servility?"

at this point, I began to envy the horse left in the stable
at this point, someone riding me started hitting my face

(1988)

INSTRUCTION
(1972–1976)

When the People Stand Up from Cheese
当人民从干酪上站起

song omits the bloodiness of revolution
August is like a cruel bow
the poison boy walks out of the commune
with tobacco and a dry throat
livestock wear barbaric blinders
blackened corpses hanging over their butts like swollen drums
until the sacrifice behind the hedge eventually blurs
and far away, more smoking troops embark

(1972)

For Whom the Bell Tolls

钟为谁鸣

—I'm asking you, telegraph building
freedom has always been as frail as a bachelor's ears
and wisdom is weak, in postnatal hibernation
education and children have their throats grabbed by dirty hands
while knowledge is like the guilty, corralled out to the hills
only time repeats the director's thoughts and predictions
on the backs of fictive newspapers
then there's you, of course, extending a silly girl's
long, long neck, smiling with anemic lips
before subconsciously wiping it away, as if wiping away
a lie that no one wants to recall

but once the bad guy's leg hair swipes the mud on the wall
the apples tied to the tree will cover the ground
everything will be totally different then
I will definitely throw my hat in the air then
and grab my "honeymoon" and slippers from beneath the bed
then there's you, of course, running up
like a simple manual laborer
in pursuit, big-jointed feet kicking wildly
at the "referee"

(1972)

Farewell

告别

the green fields are like thought that's just slackened
construction a dusk without end
when the future advances like troops
you, you will be pushed up unfamiliar country roads
walking down a side lane toward growth
the lights of ten thousand homes are one loneliness
the shepherd holds his red whip tight
guarding the night, guarding darkness —

(1972)

Blessing

祝福

when society had a breech birth
the thin, dark widow tied her talisman to a bamboo pole
and waved it at the rising moon
a blood-soaked ribbon emitting an interminable stench
it drew mad dogs from all directions barking through the night

at that superstitious hour
my country was taken off by some other father
to wander London parks and Michigan streets
to gaze at rushing footsteps with orphan eyes
and repeatedly mutter old insults and expectations

(1973)

Youth

青春

emptiness, slipping from
kissed lips, with a
previously undetected clarity:

on the street where I went in wild pursuit of women
today a worker in white gloves
is calmly spraying pesticide

(1973)

Night

夜

in a night full of symbols
the moon is like the pale face of the ill
like the shifting time of a mistake
while death is like the doctor at bedside:

dispassionate passions
the heart's fearsome variations
on the field before the house the moonlight coughs lightly
a moonlight signifying exile clear to the eye

(1973)

Auspicious Day

吉日

as if the conflict of right and wrong were settled
as if the libations had been drunk
outside the prison seeped the light of dawn
and flowers bloomed crudely
a lifetime of shame redeemed
but dreams, while vivid in memory, resounded like a bugle:

the wind does not disperse the passions of earlier years
on harvested land
under the glare of the sun
the suffering lazy villages
still have their thoughts awoken
still put free lives out to pasture —

(1973)

Could

能够

you could get drunk on gulps of liquor
could be gallant and sloshed
could worry over scattered emotions
at noon
behind the tick-tock clock window curtain
could feel embarrassment serious and long lasting

could take walks alone
sit in chairs painted green
and shut your eyes for a bit
could sigh in comfort
recalling unhappy events
forgetting where to
flick the ashes

could lose your temper
on sick days, and make a fool of yourself
could walk familiar roads
back home
could have someone kiss you
wash you up, with refined lies
awaiting you, such a life

how great it could be, wherever and whenever
hands could pluck flowers
lips could reach lips
no storms, no revolutions
the land could be irrigated by all the alcohol the people would
    donate
to live like this, how great it could be would be how great it
    would be!

(1973)

To the Sun
致太阳

give us a home, give us mottoes
you make all children ride on father's shoulders
give us light, give us shame
you make dogs wander after poets

give us time, make us labor
you sleep through the night, a pillow for our hopes
baptize us, make us believe
under your blessing, we die after birth

check peace's dreamscape and smiling visage
you are the chancellor of god
confiscating human avarice and envy
you are sovereign of souls

you love reputation, and encourage us to be brave
caressing everyone's head, you respect the common
you created, rising from the east
but are unfree, like a coin in global circulation

(1973)

Early Winter Light
入冬的光芒

tilting toward the splattered-blood gravestone
an incubus moves through the east
the sun is in dusk's earnest robes
weakening its might
a child embraces the furnace to swallow the cold
winter, the elder of the seasons
marches on, holding its corpse aloft

(1973)

Poet

诗人

draped in moonlight, I am upheld as a frail king
letting sentences like a swarm of bees rush in
to be deliberated on the body of my youth
they dig into me, cogitate me
they make me accomplish nothing

(1973)

liquor didn't fill up the poets' hope
hastily dusk inters the lamentations of yet one more day
all the passing light and time spent up in the porcelain shop
or else, this is our metropole
and all its literature

(1974)

Crows

乌鸦

like the sky above the crematorium
where the ash slowly drifts and spreads
they, dark funereal angels
at the moment of death's arrival in the world of men
flee dusk
like a swarm of musical notations

watching them go
is a silent
theater of a sky
as if countless silent past events
in pessimistic immersion
continued their passive sighs

(1974)

My Travels with Marguerite
玛格丽和我的旅行

A
like the way promises were made to the sun
Marguerite, go wild:

for you I would plunder
a thousand of Paris's most lavish jewelry shops
and wire you a hundred thousand
wet kisses from Caribbean shores
if you'd bake but one British pastry
grill two Spanish steaks
and go back to your dad's study
to steal me a pinch of Turkish tobacco
then let us stay clear
of wedding rackets
and go together to the Black Sea
to Hawaii, to marvelous Nice
with me, your funny
unfaithful lover
together, to the seashore
to the naked seashore
to the coffee-colored seashore that belongs to poets
and wander there and kiss, leaving
our straw hats and tobacco pipes and random thoughts . . .

would you, my Marguerite
go with me, to a country of passions

to a tropical city under cocoa trees

a harbor docked with golden merchant ships
where you see monkeys by the troop
binge drinking under parasols
and sailors with silver earrings
fluttering long eyelashes in the sunset
you will be surrounded by greedy businessmen
you'll earn their praise
but will earn pimply tangerines too
oh, Marguerite, you haven't seen the countless
dark women in the water
swimming like eels!

go with me
Marguerite, let us
walk to the one thousand and first resplendent Arabian night
walk to the polychromatic evenings of the Persian gulf
old people from other countries with pink skin
feed peacocks with fortified red wine
oily-skinned snake-charmers
play woodwinds in the snake forest of Calcutta
we'll find moonstones in India
and walk into a palace
a palace glittering with gold and jade
riding an elephant, advancing like a myth

B
oh, noble Marguerite
ignorant Marguerite
go with me, to the Chinese countryside
to the peaceful impoverished countryside

to go see those
honest and ancient people

those numb and unfortunate peasants
peasants, my dear
are you familiar with peasants
under the glare of the sun and of fate
suffering sons
in their black superstitious huts
living fervently for so many years

let's go there and see
melancholy Marguerite
poet Marguerite
I want you to remember forever
that painful vision
that innocent land:

a wife with a pockmarked face sacrificing thanksgiving
bathing her child, baking a holy cake
silently observing a countryside ritual
to begin the laboring people's
miserable holy supper

(1974)

Notes on Aesthetics
美学笔记

the Forbidden City drumbeat from two hundred years ago
now tends to silence, history's late-stage footsteps
yet ominously reverberate around
ten million unfathomable streams of thought
the retrogression of one soul
crosses dream's ancient room
toward the night surge of the east . . .

the gate I glimpse of divine might
shuts again, the concept
weary from voyaging, only the tree I leaned on
still hiding in the dark
like birds perched in sleep
with their feathers just slightly ruffled

(1976)

Instruction

教诲

—*a decadent memorial*

in just one night, the wound burst
and all the books on the bookshelf betrayed them
only the era's greatest singer
with a hoarse voice, at ear-side, sang softly:
    night of jazz, night of a century
they were eliminated by the forests of an advanced society
and limited to such themes:
to appear only as a foil to the
world's miseries, miseries
that would become their lives' obligation

who says the themes of their early lives
were bright, even today they still take it
as a harmful dictum
on a night with no artistic storyline
lamplight originated in misperception
what they saw was always
a monotonous rope appearing in winter's snowfall
they could only keep playing, tirelessly
wrestling with whatever flees and living
with whatever cannot remember
even if it brought back their earliest longings
emptiness became the stain on their lives

their misfortune came from the misfortune of ideals
but their pain they'd helped themselves to
self-consciousness sharpened their thinking

but from self-consciousness, blood loss
they couldn't make peace with tradition
even though the world had existed
uncleanly a long time before their birth
still they wanted to find
whichever first criminal discovered "truth"
and tear down the world
and all the time it needed to wait

faced with chains hanging around their necks
their only crazy act
was pulling them tighter
but they were no comrades
their disparate destructive forces
were never close to grabbing society's attention
and they were reduced to being spiritual criminals
because: they had abused allegory

yet in the end, they pray in the classroom of thought
and fall comatose at seeing their own handwriting so clearly:
the time they lived in was not the one the lord had arranged
they are the misborn, stopped at the point of misunderstanding
    life
and all they went through — nothing but the tragedy of being
    born

(1976)

DUO DUO became one of the founders of contemporary Chinese poetry four decades ago and remains an important voice today. A native of Beijing, he settled in the Netherlands after being exiled in 1989; he returned to China in 2004. Winner of the prestigious Neustadt International Prize for Literature in 2010, he has been described by Eliot Weinberger as "a political poet who makes no statements; a realist poet in an alternate universe."

LUCAS KLEIN is a father, writer, and translator. He is executive editor of the Hsu-Tang Library of Classical Chinese Literature from Oxford University Press, and his scholarship and criticism have appeared in the monograph *The Organization of Distance: Poetry, Translation, Chineseness* (Brill, 2018) and in *Chinese Poetry and Translation: Rights and Wrongs*, coedited with Maghiel van Crevel (Amsterdam University Press, 2019), as well as in *Comparative Literature Studies, LARB, Jacket, CLEAR, PMLA,* and other venues. His translation *Notes on the Mosquito: Selected Poems of Xi Chuan* (New Directions, 2012) won the Lucien Stryk Asian Translation Prize in 2013; other translations include the poetry of Mang Ke, *October Dedications* (Zephyr and Chinese University Press, 2018), and contributions to *Li Shangyin* (New York Review Books, 2018). His translations of the poetry of Duo Duo won a PEN/Heim Translation Fund grant. He is an associate professor of Chinese at Arizona State University.